Fascinating Womanhood

Fascinating Womanhood

By HELEN B. ANDELIN

For information regarding classes write:
FASCINATING WOMANHOOD FOUNDATION
P. O. Box 3617
Santa Barbara, California 93105

Revised Copyright 1965
Published by Pacific Press
P. O. Box 3738
Santa Barbara, California 93105

20th Printing, 1972

A WORD OF EXPLANATION BY THE AUTHOR

Many of the teachings of this book were inspired by a series
of booklets published in the 1920s, entitled *The Secrets of
Fascinating Womanhood*. These booklets have long been
out of print and the authors unknown.

Permissions:

From *The Priceless Gift*, by Eleanor Wilson McAdoo. Copyright © 1962 by Eleanor Wilson McAdoo.
Used by permission of McGraw-Hill Book Co. New York, N.Y.

From *The Ego in Love and Sexuality*, by Dr. Edrita Fried. Copyright © 1960. Reprinted by permission of
Grune and Stratton, Inc. New York 16, N.Y.

From *The Power of Sexual Surrender*, by Dr. Marie N. Robinson. Copyright © 1959 by Marie N.
Robinson. Reprinted by permission of Doubleday & Co., Inc. New York, N.Y.

From *Marriage for Moderns*, by Henry A. Bowman. Copyright © 1960 by the McGraw Hill Book Co.
Used by permission.

From *Women and Sometimes Men*, by Florida Scott-Maxwell. Copyright © 1957 by Florida Scott
Maxwell. Printed by permission of Alfred A. Knopf, Inc. New York, N.Y.

LITHOGRAPHED IN U.S.A.

Introduction

To be loved and cherished is a woman's highest goal in marriage. This book is written to restore your hope in such a goal—and to suggest principles which you must apply in winning a man's genuine love.

The Sea of Darkness

Never before in history has there been a generation of women so disillusioned, disappointed, and unhappy in marriage as in our times. Many feel that married life does not offer what they had hoped and dreamed it would. Some feel neglected, unappreciated, and often unloved. When they search for the answer why, they feel lost in a sea of darkness. Some are resigned to this condition, but others still hope and search for the answers.

There are, of course, many women who have achieved a high level of happiness. But in many cases it is not the happiness of which they once dreamed, and it falls short of their goals. They feel a need for a richer, fuller life. They too, need light and understanding.

The Greater Darkness

In this vast sea of matrimonial darkness, there are other women who are in greater darkness, for they think they are happy when they are not. They live by the side of happiness, but are strangers to her beauty. They are satisfied to eat the crumbs which fall from the table, for they have never tasted the banquet; they think the weeds are pretty, for they have never seen beautiful flowers; and some are content with hell, for they have never known heaven.

A Woman's Heaven

What is happiness in marriage for a woman? Is it to have a nice home? Happy and healthy children? A successful husband? Time for talents? No money problems? When husband and wife have fun together? Is it the feeling of being a successful homemaker? Is it to be admired by her associates?

All of these things are important, and some essential, but there is one need which is fundamental, and it is for her to be loved and cherished by her man. Without this one ingredient she is unfulfilled. She may be a successful person in many ways, and happy to a degree, but inside there will be something missing. She will not know heaven. She will enjoy weeds instead of flowers.

THE ANSWER

Is there a light to bring her out of darkness, and guide her to this earthly heaven? There is a light, and it is based upon fundamental law.

All life is governed by law. There is no such thing as chance. One woman succeeds in marriage because of obedience to law. Another fails because of disobedience to it. Neither may understand the law. Obedience is not always based upon understanding. But the result of obedience is invariably success, and disregard for it is always failure.

Through ignorance of the very simple operation of these plain laws much unnecessary unhappiness exists. We find one woman happy, admired, and loved; and another, no less attractive, no less essentially admirable, and no less loveable, neglected, unhappy, and disappointed. Why? This book tells why, for it explains the laws which she must obey if she is to be admired, loved and appreciated.

FASCINATING WOMANHOOD

Fascinating Womanhood is designed to teach women how to be happy in marriage. It will teach three essentials in creating the happy marriage.

1. *Love.* Since the cornerstone of a woman's happiness with her husband is to be loved, the essential aim of this book is to teach those principles which she must apply in arousing his deepest feelings.

Love is not reserved for the young, the single, nor the beautiful. It is reserved for those who arouse it in a man. If a man does not love with heart and soul, it is entirely the woman's fault.

A man ceases to adore and cherish a woman after marriage, because she ceases to do the things which arouse these feelings. If she obeys the laws upon which love is based, she can kindle a deep and stirring feeling within his heart.

This book will teach *The Art of Winning a Man's Complete Love and Adoration.* It isn't necessary for the man to know or do anything about the matter. In fact, it is an advantage if he does not. The art is to arouse his feelings. This is not a difficult accomplishment for woman, because it is based upon her natural instincts. In our complicated, highly civilized life of today, many of her natural instincts have become dulled or suppressed. She needs but to re-discover that which belongs to her by nature.

2. *Her desires.* Not only is love necessary to a woman, but if she is to be truly happy in marriage she must be able to have the things that are dear to her heart. She is a human being with human needs, longings and rights. So the art of getting what she wants, without causing a marital stir, is worth knowing.

3. *Human Dignity.* Also essential to her happiness in marriage is her human dignity. She cannot suffer hurt, humiliations, insults or unfair treatment by her mate without damage to her soul. She must learn how to respond so that she does not suffer. This book will teach her how to handle these difficult situations without pain, without friction. It will teach her how to act when treated unfairly or imposed on or ignored.

Within these pages I will point out those principles which she must obey if she is to be happy, loved and appreciated. My aim is to teach her how to become "The real woman", the kind she is designed to be, the kind a man wants.

A woman holds within her grasp the possibilities of a heavenly marriage. She can bring it about independently of any deliberate action on the part of her husband. So a woman holds *the keys to her own happiness.*

In accomplishing this goal, she loses none of her dignity, influence nor freedom, but gains them. And it is only then that she can play her vital part in this world.

The role of woman when played correctly is fulfilling, fascinating and full of intrigue. There never need be a dull moment. The practice of this art of womanhood is an enjoyable one and is filled with rich rewards, numerous surprises and vast happiness.

What This Book Can Do for You

It will teach you:
1. The ideal woman, from a man's point of view.
2. What men find fascinating in women.
3. How to understand men, their vulnerable points, characteristics and peculiarities.
4. How to react to a man's different moods and feelings in order to build up his confidence and respect in himself.
5. How to arouse his deepest feelings of love and tenderness.
6. How to cause a man to protect you, to do things for you and to offer you his true devotion.
7. How to obtain those things in life which mean so much—things you are justified in having and for which you are dependent upon your husband, and how to add charm and love to your marriage by doing so.
8. How to bring out the best in your husband without push or persuasion.
9. How to understand the feminine role, and the happiness which comes with its fulfillment.
10. How to understand the masculine role, the respect due this divine calling and the importance of such respect in the happiness of both husband and wife.
11. How to react when a man is thoughtless, unfair or negligent.
12. How to be attractive, even adorable when you are angry.
13. How to keep the line of communication open in marriage so that a good feeling always exists.
14. How to gain true happiness in marriage, while placing the husband's happiness as a primary goal.

Contents

CHAPTER I

Celestial Love

In the city of Agra in Northern India stands the Taj Mahal. Although it was built in the seventeenth century, it is still one of the most beautiful buildings in the world and the most costly tomb in existence. It was built by the Indian ruler Shah Jahan, in memory of his favorite wife, Mumtaz-i-Mahal which means "Pride of the Palace." Mumtaz died at the birth of her four-teenth child. The Shah had other wives, but bestowed such honor to only one—Mumtaz. Where is our Taj Mahal? Have we earned such love and devotion from our man?

What is Celestial Love? It is the holy love the Shah had for his wife. Celestial refers to love in its highest form. It lifts it out of the mediocre and places it in the heavens where love belongs. It is flowers rather than weeds—the banquet rather than the crumbs.

Do you think this type of love exists when a man tells his wife frequently that he loves her, remembers her birthday, takes her out to dinner often and is generous and kind? Not necessarily. These attentions are admirable but they are not the attributes of real love. A dutiful husband may do or say these things without any actual feelings towards his wife.

Celestial love is more intense, more spontaneous and dynamic than the passive actions just mentioned. When a man loves with all his heart there is s stirring within his soul. At times it is a feeling approaching worship for the woman. At other times he is fascinated, enchanted and amused. It has been described by some men as a feeling almost like pain. It can cause a man to feel like biting his teeth together. Along with all of these thrilling and consuming sensations, there is a tenderness, an overwhelming desire to protect and shelter his woman from all harm, danger and difficulty of life.

These feelings cause him to pour out his romantic love in words to her or to someone he trusts.

JOHN ALDEN AND PRISCILLA

An illustration of Celestial love is expressed in Longfellow's account of John Alden and Priscilla; in which John said tenderly of Priscilla:

"There is no land so sacred, no air so pure and wholesome as is the air she breathes, and the soil that is pressed by her footsteps. Here for her sake will I stay, and like an invisible presence, hover around her forever, protecting, supporting her weakness."

VICTOR HUGO'S LOVE

Another expression of man's intense love is in the following words of the author, Victor Hugo, written about the woman he loved in real life:

"Do I exist for my own personal happiness? No, my whole existence is devoted to her, even in spite of her. And by what right should I have dared to aspire to her love? What does it matter, so that it does not injure her happiness? My duty is to keep close to her steps, to surround her existence with mine, to serve her as a barrier against all dangers; to offer my head as a stepping stone, to place myself unceasingly between her and all sorrows, without claiming reward, without expecting recompense . . . Alas! If she only allow me to give my life to anticipating her every desire, all her caprices; if she but permit me to kiss with respect her adored footprints; if she but consent to lean upon me at times amidst the difficulties of life."

It might be easy for you to agree that single men might have such feelings, but what about the married man?

WOODROW WILSON

Listen to the following words written by President Woodrow Wilson to his beloved wife Ellen, after they had been married for 17 years:

"All that I am, all that has come to me in life, I owe to you . . . I could not be what I am, if I did not take such serene happiness from my union with you. You are the spring of content; and so long as I have you, and you too are happy, nothing but good and power can come to me. Ah, my incomparable little wife, may God bless and keep you."

And after being married for 28 years, he writes from the White House: "I adore you! No President but myself ever had exactly the right sort of wife! I am certainly the most fortunate man alive."

And in another letter:

"I can think of nothing, while I write, but only you. My days are not so full of anxiety and of a sense of deep responsibility as they are of you, my absent darling, who yet plays the leading part in my life every minute of the day."

These were taken from "The Priceless Gift", a collection of letters written by President Wilson to his wife Ellen. Each letter is a love letter, warm and intimate.

Some of you may believe your husbands are incapable of such feelings, or at least incapable of expressing them. This is doubtful. The warm, tender letters of President Wilson were a surprise to many who knew his personality—that of an unemotional schoolmaster. Every man has the capability of being tender, romantic, and adoring, if these passions are awakened in him by the woman.

Is it Selfish?

If you think it is selfish to want celestial love you are mistaken. Bestowing such love is a real joy to a man. And he is more of a man because of it. It helps him to excel and succeed in life. It gives him something to work for, to live for, and if necessary to die for. The woman who arouses such holy feelings brings man fulfillment. The woman who fails robs him of one of his finer joys.

And isn't celestial love what every woman has longed for since the world began? Don't you recall as a little girl the childish dream of your imagination when you were the beautiful princess who was rescued from great danger by a handsome prince charming. And didn't he plead for your hand in marriage, and offer to give his life, if necessary, to make you happy? Let us return to the dream of our youth, for it is celestial love.

What are the qualities that inspire celestial love in man's heart? To know we must learn the principles upon which love is based. We must study "The Kind of Woman a Man Wants", the kind which awakens his emotions of worship, adoration and love.

For a true state of celestial love to exist, woman must love her man deeply in return. The same principles which awaken love in man's heart will cause a woman to love and admire her man.

CHAPTER II

"The Ideal Woman" from a Man's Point of View

In order to understand man's choice of an ideal, we must see woman through man's eyes. We must rid ourselves of all preconceived ideas, thoughts, and standards of feminine charm. We do not know what men want—for we are not men. Their standards of feminine perfection are entirely different than our own.

The things that we women admire in each other are rarely attractive to men. On the other hand, the characteristics which the average woman ignores, or condemns in another woman, are sometimes just the characteristics which make her fascinating to men. *Women are blind to their own charms,* which is the very reason it is often difficult for them to realize what a man wants.

This difference in viewpoint is illustrated in Thackeray's *Vanity Fair.* For example, Amelia, one of the leading characters, was not admired by the women of her acquaintance. "She is facade and insipid," remarks one lady, and another asks, "What could George find in that creature?" Then Thackeray adds a few observations of his own.

"Has the loved reader, in his experience of society never heard similar remarks by good natured female friends; who always wonder what you could see in Miss Smith that is so fascinating; or what could induce Major Jones to propose to that silly, insignificant, simpering Miss Thompson."

And what do the men think of Amelia? They consider her a "kind, fresh, smiling, artless, tender little domestic goddess whom men are inclined to worship."

Haven't you been puzzled at times to know what a certain man sees in a particular woman? To you she doesn't hold any appeal, yet the man may be completely enamored. The fascination men feel for certain women seems an eternal riddle to the rest of us. Even when asked "Why", the man finds himself at a loss to explain the spell cast upon him.

And haven't you also known women who appear to have all the qualities which ought to please a man, yet they are unnoticed, neglected and often unloved? I know a young girl who was losing her husband to another woman, and upon discovering it, looked in the mirror and said to herself, "I can't find a thing wrong with you." She was blind to her own lack. She could not see the missing ingredients, because she was looking at herself through a woman's eyes.

This blindness on the part of woman is why we spend countless hours on our appearance and may still fail to be fascinating to men. And when we reach into middle age, we dread to contemplate wrinkles, and sagging muscles, both of which will inevitably come in spite of all efforts. We cling to the false idea that we are losing our beauty and will lose our husbands admiration along with it. If we would only realize that real feminine charm is enduring.

Appearance is important but not all important. A woman must have a lot more to offer a man than an attractive outer shell if she is to win his heart. If you will observe, you will see many stunning women who have lost their men. And if you will look further you will see others who are not particularly attractive, as we women see it, and yet they possess their man's wholehearted devotion.

In our study of the kind of woman a man wants, we must remember then that he judges with a different set of values. What are his values, and what does he find ideal in woman?

I am going to try to create this ideal in your mind, the IDEAL WOMAN, from a man's point of view. You cannot work for a goal if you do not know what that goal is. You must have an image, or a mental picture of the woman you ought to be—the kind a man wants. Once you have this picture firmly established you will be drawn to it. You will tend to *be* this image, or this ideal.

"But," you may ask, "doesn't this ideal differ in each man?" Of course men do have different tastes. Some men want a woman who is quiet and retiring, others prefer one who is dashing and outgoing, and still others want a more dramatic or glamorous type. Some men like tall blondes, others prefer short brunettes. Some appreciate a woman's ability to cook and sew, while others insist a sense of humor is more essential. There are many different types of men in the world, and they don't all want the same kind of woman. But with all their differences men are still alike in their basic desires. There are certain qualities which have universal attraction and only certain ones will arouse their love. It is these qualities which we will analyze in our ideal of women.

THE ANGELIC AND THE HUMAN

The ideal woman from a man's view point is divided into two parts. The one part is her spiritual qualifications. We will call this side of her the Angelic. The other part relates to her Human characteristics. We will call this side of her Human.

Angelic	Human
Arouses a feeling near worship	Fascinates, Amuses
Brings man deep abiding happiness	Arouses a desire to protect and shelter

TOGETHER HE CHERISHES

Together these two distinct qualities blended into one whole offer the perfect woman, from a man's viewpoint. They are both essential in winning his complete love.

These two separate qualities arouse different feelings within a man's heart. The Angelic arouses a feeling so holy that it approaches worship. The Human side, which is just as essential, fascinates and amuses man. The Angelic brings man deep happiness, while the Human arouses in his heart a tender feeling, a desire to protect and shelter. Together the feeling is one of cherishing a woman.

When a woman has both the Angelic and the Human characteristics she wins man's heart and soul. This is the kind of woman he loves more than life itself, and yet at the same time she gives his life purpose and character.

"DAVID COPPERFIELD"

A perfect illustration of the Angelic and the Human in Woman is in the story of David Copperfield, by Charles Dickens. Our ideal, however, is not represented by one woman, but by two, Agnes and Dora.

AGNES

Agnes represents the Angelic side of our ideal, the side which inspires worship. David Copperfield knew Agnes from childhood and worshipped her from the time he first beheld her. The following description of their first meeting describes his reverent feeling.

"Mr Wickfield, (Agnes' father) tapped at a door in a corner of the paneled wall, and a girl of about my age came quickly out and kissed him. On her face I saw immediately the placid and sweet expression of the lady whose picture had looked at me downstairs, (her mother). It seemed to my imagination as if the portrait had grown womanly and the original remained a child. Although her face was quite bright and happy, there was a tranquility about it, and about her—a quiet, good, calm spirit—that I never have forgotten; that I never shall forget. 'This was his little housekeeper, his daughter, Agnes.' Mr. Wickfield said. When I heard how he said it, and saw how he held her hand, I guessed what the one motive of his life was. She had a little basket trifle hanging at her side with keys in it, and she looked as staid, and as discreet a housekeeper as the old house could have. She listened to her father as he told her about me, with a pleasant face; and when he had concluded, proposed to my aunt that we should go upstairs and see my room. We all went up together, she before us. A glorious old room it was with more oak beams and diamond panes; and the broad balustrade going all the way up.

"I cannot call to mind where or when, in my childhood, I

had seen a stained-glass window in a church. Nor do I recall its subject. But I know that when I saw her turn around in the grave light of the old staircase, and wait for me above, I thought of that window; and I associated something of its tranquil brightness with Agnes Wickfield ever afterwards."

David and Agnes became the closest of friends. She gave him comfort, understanding, true sympathy and comradeship. "As if," he writes, "In love, joy, sorrow, hope, or disappointment, in all emotions, my heart turned naturally there, and found its refuge and best friend."

Agnes always had a sacred, and a peaceful influence on David. At one time, while under great stress and tension, he said, "Somehow, as I wrote to Agnes on a fine evening by my open window, and the remembrance of her clear calm eyes and gentle face came stealing over me, it shed such a peaceful influence upon the hurry and agitation in which I had been living lately . . . that it soothed me into tears."

But although he had known Agnes since childhood, although he had worshipped her from the time he first beheld her, and although he senses all along that she alone is equipped to give him true sympathy and comradeship, he becomes madly infatuated, not with Agnes, but with Dora.

DORA

Dora represents the Human side of our ideal, the side that fascinates, captivates, and inspires an overwhelming tenderness in a man's heart and a desire to protect and shelter. David describes her in the following words:

"She was a fairy, and a sylph. She was more than human to me. I don't know what she was—anything that no one ever saw, and everything that everybody ever wanted.

"She had the most delightful little voice, the gayest little laugh, the pleasantest and most fascinating little ways that ever led a lost youth into hopeless slavery.

"She was rather diminutive altogether . . . she was too bewildering. To see her lay the flowers against her dimpled chin was to lose all presence of mind and power of language in feeble ecstacy."

Her child-like ways, her dear little whims, and caprices, her girlish trust in him, her absolute dependency upon others to

provide for her, make an irresistable appeal to David's gentle-
manly and chivalrous heart.

She fascinated him, for he writes: "I could only sit down
before the fire, biting the key of my carpet bag, and think of the
captivating, girlish, bright eyed, lovely Dora. What a form she
had, what a face she had, what a graceful, variable, enchanting
manner."

MARRIED TO DORA, DAVID TURNS TO AGNES

Yet even while such feelings toward Dora are at their highest
he misses the comfort, the understanding, the appreciation, and
the sacred influences of Agnes.

"Dora," he tells Agnes, "is rather difficult to—I would not
for the world say, to rely upon, because she is the soul of purity
and truth—but rather difficult to—I hardly know how to express it. Whenever I have not had you, Agnes, to advise and
approve in the beginning, I have seemed to go wild, and to get
into all sorts of difficulty. When I have come to you, at last, (as
I have always done) I have come to peace and happiness."

DORA'S HOMEMAKING

In marriage, Dora also failed as a homemaker. Their home
was in a constant clutter:

"I could not have wished for a prettier little wife at the opposite end of the table, but I certainly could have wished when
we sat down for a little more room. I did not know how it was,
but although there were only two of us, we were at once always
cramped for room, and yet had always enough to lose everything in. I suspect it could have been because nothing had a
place of its own."

Dora could not manage the household finances, nor the
household help, although she tried. Nor could she cook, although David bought her an expensive cook book. But she used
the book to let her little dog stand on.

THE VOID IN HIS LIFE

While married to Dora he continued to love her. She fascinated and amused him, and he felt tenderly towards her. But it
was not a complete love, nor did it bring him real genuine happiness, for he said:

"I loved my wife dearly, and I was happy; but the happiness I had vaguely anticipated once was not the happiness I enjoyed, and there was something wanting. An unhappy feeling pervaded my life, as a strain of sorrowful music, faintly heard in the night." And he said, "I wished my wife had had more character and purpose to sustain me; had been endowed with a power to fill up the void which somewhere seemed to be about me." Later on in the story Dora died and David turned to Agnes.

When married to Agnes, David enjoyed real peace and happiness, for she filled up the void in his life. She was a wonderful homemaker, and gave him true understanding. They had children and a wonderful home life. His love for Agnes was holy, but it was not complete. During his marriage to Agnes he still had tender recollections of Dora that played upon his emotions. In thinking of her he writes:

"This appeal of Dora's made such a strong impression on me . . . I look back on the time I write of; I invoke the innocent figure that I dearly loved to come out from the mists and shadows of the past, and turn its gentle head toward me once again."

On one occasion his little girl came running in to her father with a ring on her finger very much like the engagement ring he had given to Dora. The little ring—a band of forget-me-knots with blue stones, so reminded him of Dora, that, he said, "there was a momentary stirring in my heart, like pain!"

COMPARING THE TWO

If Agnes had had the girlishness, the adorably human and childlike manner of Dora, and her complete dependency upon man for protection and guidance, David would never have made the mistake of marrying another. His worship for Agnes would have turned into genuine love, into the desire to protect and shelter. On the other hand, if Dora had had the sympathetic understanding, the appreciation of his highest ideals, and the depth of character that Agnes had, and had given his home a semblance of order, David's mad infatuation for her would have developed into everlasting adoration and love. Neither of the two, unfortunate for them, represents the whole of the Angelic and the Human. Each of them made mistakes, each of them won and lost David, but each of them is well worth emulating in some respects.

ANALYZING AGNES

What she had

Agnes had four outstanding qualities that appeal to men, and they are all on the Angelic side of our ideal.

1. *She had a pure and lovely character,* for David always associated her with a "stained glass window of a church," and said she had a sacred influence on him. Perhaps the greatest test of her character came when David married Dora. Even though Agnes herself loved David, she did not become bitter or revengeful toward either of them, but continued her unselfish friendship to David, and became a friend to Dora as well. She had the courage to keep her love a secret and to live a useful life in spite of her own disappointment. Further evidence of her character is shown in her devotion to her father and the sacrifice of many of her own pleasures for his sake.

2. *Agnes understood men.* She gave David true understanding. She knew how to rejoice with him in his triumphs and sympathize with him in his difficulties. She brought him comfort, peace, and comradeship.

3. *She was a capable housekeeper.* From the time she was a child, Agnes was a "discreet little housekeeper." She took care of the meals, the house, and her father with womanly efficiency.

4. *Inner happiness.* As a result of her pure character, Agnes had a "tranquility about her, and a good calm spirit," which indicates peace, or happiness within.

What Agnes Lacked

1. *She was too independent.* She was too hesitant to lean on him or to need him. She was too unselfish, for David said: "Agnes, ever my guide and best support—if you had been more mindful of yourself, and less of me, when we grew up together, I think my heedless fancy never would have wandered from you."

Because she hesitated to lean on him for anything, this made her appear to be independent. She didn't appear to need his manly care and protection.

2. *She lacked the girlish, childlike, trusting qualities.*

3. *She lacked the gentle, tender, fascinating little ways that stir a man's heart.*

ANALYZING DORA

What she had:

1. *She had an enchanting manner.*
2. *She was childlike, girlish.* At times he would refer to her as his "child-bride." At times she would shake her curls as little girls do. Her attitude was childlike, trusting.
3. *She had tender little ways.* The way she laid the flowers against her dimpled chin, or the way she patted the horses or spanked her little dog fascinated David.
4. *She was gay.* She had a gay little laugh, a delightful little voice, and the pleasantest little ways.
5. *She was bright eyed.*
6. *She was dependent.* She was helplessly in need of masculine protection and guidance. She had a girlish trust in David.

What Dora Lacked.

1. *She was a poor homemaker.* She could neither keep house, nor cook, nor manage her household expenses.
2. *She lacked character.* Dora was good, pure and kind, but she was very self-centered. David said, "I wished my wife had had more character and purpose to sustain me by." She was too absorbed in her own little problems, cares, and whims to make a good wife.
3. *She did not understand men.* This was her greatest lack. She did not know how to offer sympathy, understanding, appreciation, or intellectual comradeship, for he writes, "It would have been better if my wife could have helped me more, and shared my many thoughts in which I had no partner."

THE FEELING DAVID HAD FOR EACH OF THEM

The feeling David had for Agnes was one near worship. She had a sacred influence on him. She brought him peace and happiness, and without her he seemed to "go wild and get into difficulty." Thinking about her "soothed him into tears." He felt as though she were a part of him, "as one of the elements of my natural home."

The feeling he had for Dora was different. She fascinated and amused him; "she was more than human to me";"She was a fairy and a sylph"; "I don't know what she was—anything that no one ever saw and everything that everybody ever wanted." All of her delicate and bright mannerisms aroused his irresistable longing to shelter and protect her.

I would like to stress that David Copperfield felt two distinctly different types of love for these two girls. David experienced a type of love for Agnes all along, but it was not strong enough to bring him to marriage. And even though this type of love brings men the greatest peace and the truest and most abiding happiness—it is not the most driving.

The kind of love David felt for Dora was forceful, consuming and intense. He felt like "biting the key of his carpet bag" when he thought of her; he was "in fairyland." He was "a captive and a slave."

This type of love, however, was not complete, nor did it bring him real happiness, for he said, "I loved my wife dearly, and I was happy; but the happiness I vaguely anticipated once was not the happiness I enjoyed and there was something wanting. An unhappy feeling pervaded my life, as a strain of sorrowful music, faintly heard in the night."

While married to Agnes he experienced peace and happiness and he loved her dearly, but he still had tender recollections of Dora which sent stirring feelings through his heart.

David Copperfield never had the satisfaction of loving completely, for his feelings were inspired by two different women. Neither was the whole of our ideal, so neither could arouse his love in a complete sense.

There are many women such as Agnes in this life—women with inspiring characters. They are wonderful mothers, wonderful homemakers, and good citizens. They may be greatly appreciated and respected by their husbands, but if they lack the adorably human qualities that so fascinate men, they will not win the complete love and adoration of their husbands. A man wants more than an angel.

On the other hand, there are some women such as Dora, who are tender, childlike and gay little creatures, but if they have not the depth of character and purpose, if they are too self-centered to be good homemakers and mothers, and if they lack the ability to understand men, they will only win a part of a man's heart.

There is no reason why a woman cannot be both an Agnes and a Dora, for the Angelic and the Human qualities do not conflict. Both are a natural part of femininity and are essential to real feminine charm.

Both the Angelic and the Human qualities are essential if man is to offer you his heart and soul. Therefore, your complete happiness in marriage depends upon your development of both sides of our ideal.

DERUCHETTE

An example of a girl who had both the Angelic and Human qualities is Deruchette, heroine of the novel, *Toilers of the Sea*, by Victor Hugo:

"Her presence lights the home; her approach is like a cheerful warmth; she passes by, and we are content; she stays awhile and we are happy—Is it not a thing of divine, to have a smile which, none know how, has the power to lighten the weight of that enormous chain that all the living, in common, drag behind them? Deruchette possessed this smile; we may say that this smile was Deruchette herself.

"Deruchette had at times, an air of bewitching languor, and certain mischief in the eye, which were altogether involuntary. Sweetness and goodness reigned throughout her person; her occupation was only to live her daily life; her accomplishments were the knowledge of a few songs; her intelluctual gifts were summed up in simple innocence; she had the graceful repose of the West Indian woman, mingled at times with giddiness and vivacity, with the teasing playfulness of a child, yet with a dash of melancholy. Add to all this an open brow, a neck supple and graceful, chestnut hair, a fair skin, slightly freckled, with exposure to the sun, a mouth somewhat large, but well defined, and visited from time to time with a dangerous smile. This was Deruchette."

There is in this world no function more important than that of being charming—to shed joy around, to cast light upon dark days, to be the golden thread of our destiny, and the very spirit of grace and harmony. Is not this to render a service?

In another place Hugo says that "she who is one day to be a mother, remains for a long while a child." And when she becomes a maiden, "she is fresh and joyous as a lark." "She makes all kinds of gentle noises, murmurings of unspeakable delight to certain ears." She is, as it were, "a thread of gold, interwoven in your sombre thoughts." Further evidence of her noble qualities are found in the proposal to Deruchette by the young clergyman in the story:

"There is for me but one woman on earth. It is you. I think of you as a prayer—you are a glory in my eyes. To me, you are holy innocence. You alone are supreme. You are the living form of a benediction."

ANALYZING DERUCHETTE

Her Angelic Qualities

1. *Her character*: "Sweetness and Goodness reigned throughout her person." She had a character which was mindful of the needs of others, for she "cast light upon dark days," and had "a smile which had the power to lighten that enormous chain." Further evidence of her character is in her lover's statement that she is "holy innocence," "is like a prayer," and the "living form of a benediction."

2. *Domestic*: She was capable in her domestic duties, for "her occupation is only to live her daily life" and "her presence lights the home."

3. *Inner Happiness*: Similar to Agnes, Deruchette possessed inner happiness, or she couldn't possibly have had such ability to radiate it to others.

Her Human Qualities

1. *Childlikeness:* Like Dora, Deruchette had childlike ways. "She who is one day to be a mother, remains for a long while a child." She had a "childlike prattle," and "certain mischief in the eye," and at times "the giddiness and vivacity, and the teasing playfulness of a child."

2. *Changefulness*: Deruchette was not at all times the same. Sometimes she was radiantly happy and full of giddiness and vivacity; at other times she had an air of "bewitching languor." Although she was sweet and good, at times she had "a certain mischief in the eye." Sometimes she was full of teasing-playfulness, and at other times, "a dash of melancholy."

But changefulness, as you will learn in a later chapter, is also a childlike quality.

3. *Fresh appearance:* "She is *fresh* and joyous as the lark."

4. *Gentle:* Her gentle qualities are described in her voice: "She makes all kinds of gentle noises, murmurings of unspeakable delight."

5. *Radiates Happiness*: The most notable quality she had was her ability to radiate happiness. This was a part of her character, manner, and actions:

    a. She was fresh and joyous as the lark.
    b. She shed joy around.
    c. Cast light upon dark days.
    d. Her presence lights the home.
    e. Her approach is like a cheerful warmth.
    f. She passes by and we are content.
    g. She stays awhile and we are happy.
    h. She has a smile which had the power to lighten the weight of that enormous chain which all the living in common drag behind them—a dangerous smile, which was Deruchette herself.
    i. At times she had giddiness and vivacity.

6. *Grace*: Not mentioned before, but similar to gentleness and tenderness is that of grace. Deruchette was the very spirit of grace and harmony, and had "the graceful repose of the West Indian woman." Her neck was supple and graceful.

AMELIA

Another example in literature of a girl who was both Angelic and Human is Amelia, from the novel, *Vanity Fair*, by Thackeray.

Thackeray says that Amelia is a "kind, fresh, smiling, artless, tender little domestic goddess, whom men are inclined to worship." A few pages further he calls her "poor, little, tender heart." In another place he attributes to her "such a kindly, smiling, tender, generous heart of her own." He admits that others might not consider her beautiful:

"Indeed, I am afraid that her nose was rather short, than otherwise, and her cheeks a great deal too round for a heroine; but her face blushed with rosy health, and her lips with the freshest of smiles, and she had a pair of eyes which sparkled with the brightest and honestest of good humor, except indeed when they filled with tears, and that was a great deal too often; for the silly thing would cry over a dead canary, or over a mouse that the cat haply had seized upon; or over the end of a novel, were it ever so stupid."

Amelia had a "sweet, fresh little voice." She was subject to "little cares, fears, tears, timid misgivings." She trembled when anyone was harsh. Altogether, she was: "Too modest, too tender, too trustful, too weak, too much woman" for any man to know without feeling called upon to protect and to cherish.

ANALYZING AMELIA

Amelia had several qualities worthy of our attention.

Her Angelic Qualities

1. *Her Character:* She had a generous heart and was kindly, and since "men are inclined to worship her," she evidently had a worthy character.

2. *Her Domestic Qualities:* Thackeray calls her "a little domestic goddess."

Her Human Qualities

1. *Her freshness:* She had the freshest of smiles, and her face blushed with rosy health. She had a pair of eyes that sparkled. She had a sweet, fresh little voice.

2. *She had childlike emotions:*
Her eyes would often fill with tears.
She would cry over a dead canary, or a mouse, or a novel.
She is subject to little cares, tears, fears, timid misgivings.
She trembles when anyone is harsh.

3. *Tenderness:* She was a "tender little domestic goddess." She was "too tender, too weak, too much woman."

4. *Trustfulness:* "She was too trustful."

SUMMARY

As we come to the end of our study of these four women, we can see that there are many qualities which men admire in women. Now, I am going to blend these appealing qualities into one whole, the total woman, the kind man is inclined to worship, to protect and to cherish.

On the following page is a diagram of the ideal woman, with the essential qualities which men find appealing. Although she is divided, you should always think of her as one, the angelic and the human combined. Together they form the ultimate in real feminine charm.

Angela Human

The Ideal Woman, from a Man's Point of View

Angelic Qualities	*Human Qualities*
1. Understands Men	1. Femininity
2. Has Deep Inner Happiness	2. Radiates Happiness
3. Has a worthy character	3. Fresh Appearance and Manner
4. Is a Domestic Goddess	4. Childlikeness

The Angelic side of woman arouses in man a feeling approaching worship. These qualities bring peace and happiness to man.

The Human side of woman fascinates, amuses, captivates and enchants man. It arouses a desire to protect and shelter.

Together He Cherishes
Both Are Essential to His Celestial Love

The Angelic is what a woman *is*, and has to do with her character.

The Human is what a woman *does* and has to do with her appearance, manner, and actions.

DIFFERENCES

As I have stated, men and women differ in opinions of "the ideal woman." Women are inclined to appreciate poise, talent, intellectual gifts and cleverness of personality, whereas men admire girlishness, tenderness, sweetness of character, vivacity and the woman's ability to understand men.

A marked difference is in regards to appearance. Women are inclined to be attracted to artistic beauty such as the shape of the face, the nose and artistic clothes. Men, however, have a different interpretation of "what makes a woman beautiful." They place more stress on the sparkle in the eyes, smiles, freshness, radiance and the feminine manner, such as described by the authors in this chapter.

It is interesting to note that none of these authors placed importance upon natural beauty. Amelia and Deruchette were not beautiful girls. Amelia, for example, was chubby and stout, with a very imperfect nose—"her nose was rather short than otherwise—and her cheeks a great deal too round for a heroine." Deruchette's complexion was marred by freckles and her mouth was too large for perfection. So far are the authors from claiming beauty for these young charmers that aside from pointing out the defects mentioned, they make no attempt to describe outward appearance. Agnes and Dora were both beautiful girls. David's choice was based upon other qualities. Admitting this difference, we will have to rely on men's opinions in guiding us to what they admire in women.

You may wonder, "How do I know if these qualities are charming to men? How can I prove these things to be true?"

I must warn you—if you ask the average man to define the ideal woman you are apt to be disappointed. He may feel at a loss to describe his feelings in words. He only knows a charming quality when he sees it in action. It takes an author, such as I have referred to in these illustrations from classic literature, to skillfully describe these attributes.

"But," you may ask, "can the opinions of a few authors establish these things as true?" If you are still in doubt, *try acquiring these qualities and see for yourself the response in your husband.*

Part I

THE ANGELIC QUALITIES

1. *Understands Men*

2. *Has Deep Inner Happiness*

3. *Has a Worthy Character*

4. *Is a Domestic Goddess*

The Angelic arouses in man a feeling near worship, and brings him peace and happiness.

The Angelic side is *what a woman is*, and has to do with her spiritual qualities, or her character. They inspire in man a feeling of worship and bring him peace and happiness.

To be "The Ideal Woman," from a Man's Point of View, you must possess the Angelic as well as the Human qualities. No man completely loves a woman who is not somewhat of an angel. A woman less angelic might fascinate him or captivate him, but he will not feel for her love in all its fullness—Celestial Love.

These four qualities are separate, and yet they are one, for they are all spiritual. The following chapters in Part I are devoted to a study of these Angelic Qualities and how to acquire them.

UNDERSTANDING MEN

A man wants a woman who understands him. *But* men are not easy to understand, for they are different from women—so different in nature and temperament that it is almost as though they came from another planet.

Men don't think like we do, approach a problem in the same light, nor do they have the same sense of values or the same needs as we do. Even those needs which may be similar in man and woman differ widely in their essential value. For example: Love is essential to both. To be admired is essential to both. *But to be loved is more important to a woman and to be admired is vital to a man.* Because we fail to understand these differences, we often become baffled in our relationship with man.

AGNES

Agnes had the ability to understand men, for David said: "Whenever I have not had you, Agnes, to advise and approve in the beginning, I have seemed to go wild, and to get into all sorts of difficulty. When I have come to you, at last, as I have always done, I have come to peace and happiness." And in another place, "As if, in love, joy, sorrow, hope, or disappointment, in all emotions, my heart turned naturally there, and found its refuge and best friend."

DORA

Dora did not have this ability to understand men, for David writes: "I did sometimes feel, for a little while, that I could have wished my wife had been my counselor; . . . had been endowed with power to fill up the void which somewhere seemed to be about me." And further on: "It would have been better for me if my wife could have helped me more, and shared my many thoughts in which I had no partner."

If we are to gain an understanding of men we must know something about them. No public speaker would gain the interest of an audience that was strange to him. He wouldn't know how to begin. Neither would an advertising man try to write an advertisement unless he first knew something about the kind of people his product must interest. The better the speaker or the more the advertising man knows his audience, its peculiarities, ambitions, prejudices, opinions, and weaknesses, the more able he is to do and say the things that will prove effective.

The same is true with woman. The better she understands a man's characteristics, peculiarities, needs, and vulnerable points, the better she will know how to do and say the things that will please him. A study of these masculine characteristics is enlightening, and will be given in the following eight chapters.

CHAPTER III

Accept a Man at Face Value

If you want to win a man's heart, you must be willing to accept him at face value *and not try to change him.*

A few years ago Norman Vincent Peale, author of *The Power of Positive Thinking*, delivered an impressive lecture before a large audience. After the lecture, as was customary with Dr. Peale, he allowed time for questions which he answered over the pulpit.

One of these questions written by a woman went something like this, "I have tried to make a good home, be a good mother, and a devoted wife, but things have not worked out very well. The trouble is that my husband has not put forth equal effort to make our marriage successful."

Then she listed many of his faults, some of which were, "He neglects his children, spends money foolishly, drinks, is cross, and difficult to live with." Her question to Dr. Peale was this, "After 25 years of marriage is there any hope that he will change?"

One couldn't help but sympathize with this woman who apparently had not given up hope. While anticipating the answer, I thought to myself, "He will probably give her a lecture on 'The power of positive thinking,' and tell her to not give up hope," but to my surprise he gave no such answer.

Dr. Peale looked sternly at the audience and said with aggravation in his voice, *"Don't you know that you should always be willing to accept a man at face value and never try to change him?"*

This truthful message should be known to women everywhere. No other quality is so vital, so fundamental. It is the foundation of understanding men. *You must accept a man at face value, or you cannot win his celestial love.*

WHAT DOES FACE VALUE MEAN?

In the business world, it has a specific meaning. It is the amount a bond or an insurance policy, etc., is worth today or now. If held for a number of years it would or could be worth a good deal more, but it does have a specific value now. And what does face value mean in reference to a man? It means what he is worth today, just as he exists now, with no changes made.

What does "Accept a Man at Face Value Mean?"

It means that we recognize him as a human being who, like ourselves and all other humans, is part virtue and part fault. It is a very honest approach. We realize that the faults are there, but we are not concerned about them, for we accept the total man. If he wants to change on his own that is his business. We are satisfied with him as he is.

Acceptance does not mean tolerance—that we realize he has serious faults, but we will "put up with them." Nor does it mean dishonesty—that we must convince ourselves that he is perfect, even though he is not. Nor does it mean resignation.

When you accept a man you see him as a total man, and are content with what you see and prove your contentment by *not trying to change him.*

Yet women everywhere are trying to change their husbands. A young woman confessed to me that soon after marriage she began making a long list of her husband's faults which she had every intention of changing. She thought it was her duty to improve him.

How Women Try to Change or Improve their Husbands

In which ways do women try to improve their men? They fall into several different categories and are as follows:

1. *Personal Habits*: There are such things as poor eating habits from a nutritional standpoint, poor table manners, neglect of his appearance, poor spelling and grammar, bad temper, depressed moods, careless driving, untidy habits—especially in leaving things around the house and failure to hang up things or put things away in the proper place, lack of courtesy, swearing, smoking and drinking.

2. *How He Spends His Time*: Many women make an effort to change their husband's use of his time to better advantage. They complain that their men spend too much time away from home with the boys, in sporting events, church responsibility

and other outside activities, spend too much time watching T.V., or napping on the couch, or in the bathroom. Some complain that their husbands have too many "irons in the fire" which cause them to be always in a hurry. Many men fail to come home on time, or to bother to call their wives when they are going to be late.

3. *Duties*: Most women make an appeal to men when they fail to perform their home duties—such things as neglect of home repairs, yard work, painting and fixing. Some women complain that their men are undependable on their jobs and fail to follow through, that they fail to pay bills and neglect church duties and other duties, and that they are lazy, shiftless and therefore unsuccessful.

4. *Social Behavior*: Some wives complain that their husbands brag too much in public, talk too much, others talk too little, and many do not say the right things and are careless in their conversation. Others don't treat people properly, lacking courtesy, and many men do not select friends that please his wife and also fail to appreciate the friends which the wife chooses.

5. *Desires and Dreams*: Many women complain about their husbands aspirations and say that they have no ambition or zest for living, that they underestimate themselves, do not have a desire to better themselves. Some cannot make up their minds what they want out of life and move from one dream to another, others have no imagination and let the world go by without them. Some men's dreams are too wild and impossible to fulfill.

6. *Manly Accomplishments*: Some women urge their men to be more successful, as other men are. Some complain that their husbands fail to lead and guide their families, are indecisive, worry too much about past mistakes, are too hasty in judgment without finding out the facts, and do not have good ideas.

7. *Money*: A majority of wives complain that their men do not manage money well, spend money foolishly, are stingy with money and spend large amounts without consulting his wife.

8. *Neglect of Children*: Women make appeals to men to take more responsibility in the care and training of the children.

9. *Religion*: Women often complain that their husbands will not attend church, will not listen to their religious ideas, and are not interested in religion.

Where can we find the perfect man?

WHY DO WOMEN TRY TO CHANGE THEIR MEN?

In many instances it is because women become irritated with their men. They have not accepted them at face value and therefore find their faults difficult to live with. But more frequently, and especially among women of high caliber, it is *"for his own good."* These women say, "If you really love and care about someone, it is important to see that they get the best out of life." Therefore, I must change my husband for his own good.

If a man is truly blind to his own mistakes, and this blindness causes him to get into difficulty or fail to reach success, it is important for his wife to wake him up. But once he realizes his mistake, and if he chooses to continue making it, she should not persist in the matter. "But," his wife might say, "my husband's faults are robbing him of basic happiness; therefore, I must change him so that he can be happy." This seems like a noble aim. What possible reason could we have against it? There are four reasons why women should not try to change men and they are the following:

1. It causes marriage problems.
2. It can destroy love.
3. It doesn't work.
4. It can cause a man to rebel.

1. *It Creates Marriage Problems*

Even though a wife may set out to remake her husband with the best of intentions, it can set in motion marriage problems which can become serious.

In the first place, it can create a terrible tension in the household. The wife may suffer tension because of her concern for her husband's faults. She may worry about the consequences of his behavior. Then when she sets out to change him she creates additional tension in that he resists the change. Children too suffer when they become aware of the tension existing between the parents.

Another problem created by trying to change a man is that it crushes his ego. A man is proud in spirit. He knows his weaknesses, but he wants you to think of his better side. Remember, the important element in a man's happiness is admiration from his wife. This is his daily bread. Your suggestions that he is not acceptable threatens his security just as you would be made to feel insecure if you felt that he didn't love you.

Also, pushy suggestions and efforts to remake a man often irritate him and make his life unbearable. Often he will escape his unhappy feelings by spending time away from home in the company of others or in pleasures which compensate for his misery.

Still another problem which can occur is that of a wedge which can grow between man and wife, cutting off communication between them. The husband may become distant and withdrawn. He may live in the same house with his wife but seldom speak to her. Often this lack of communication on the part of the husband can be traced to his feeling that he is not accepted at face value.

It is difficult, if not impossible for a man to feel tenderly towards the woman who pushes him. Often the man himself does not understand his resentment towards being pushed and therefore is at a loss to explain his cooled attitude towards his wife.

The tension, resentments, lack of communication and cooled attitudes which can occur in a household because of the wife's initiative in trying to change her husband should cause her to question "if her objectives are worth it." Does what she hope to accomplish in changing her husband stack up against a peaceful home atmosphere and a good marriage relationship. Which is more important to the children, to herself and to her husband? It is doubtful that any effort a woman makes to perfect her husband is more important than love and harmony between husband and wife. And nothing is so essential to the well being and development of the children as happy parents.

2. *It Can Destroy Love*

In severe cases love itself can be destroyed. When a wife constantly pushes or nettles her husband, it is like the bite of a poisonous snake and can cause the destruction of a could-be holy marriage. One of the most tragic cases in history is that of the Russian novelist, Count Leo Tolstoi and his wife.

TOLSTOI

In the beginning of their marriage, Tolstoi and his wife were so blissfully happy that, kneeling together they prayed to God to continue the ecstasy that was theirs.

Tolstoi is one of the most famous novelists of all time. Two of his masterpieces, *War and Peace* and *Anna Karenina,* are considered literary treasures. He was so admired by his people that they followed him around day and night and took down in shorthand every word he uttered.

Although he was a man of wealth and fame, after studying the teachings of Jesus, he gave away his property, worked in the fields chopping wood, and pitching hay, made his own shoes, ate out of a wooden bowl, and tried to love his enemies. He gave away the publishing rights to his books and had the courage of his convictions to live a life he believed in.

But his wife never accepted him or his simple philosophy of life. She loved luxury and he despised it. She craved fame and the esteem of society, but these things meant nothing to him. She longed for money and riches, but he thought these things a sin. For years she made every effort to change him and his views. She screamed at him because he insisted on giving away the publishing right to his books. When he opposed her she threw herself into fits of hysteria, threatening to kill herself or jump down the well.

After 48 years, this man who had adored his wife when he married her could hardly bear the sight of her. And one of the most tragic scenes was when Countess Tolstoi, heartbroken and old and starving for affection would kneel at her husband's feet and beg him to read aloud the exquisite love passages that he had written about her in his diary fifty years previously. And as he read of those beautiful happy days that were now gone forever, both of them wept. His dying request was that she should not be permitted to come into his presence.

3. *It Doesn't Work*

Men do not change by being pushed and nettled. If women's efforts to change their men really worked, there would be some merit in it, but it is a poor approach doomed to failure. Did Tolstoi change? Did he heed his wife's suggestions? No! He opposed them to his dying day. Men do not change in this way!

"But," you might say, "I know a woman who tried to change

her husband, and she was successful." Don't let this mislead you. If you will examine the matter carefully, you will find that he changed, not due to his wife's persuasion, but because he found another incentive for changing—one that she doesn't realize. And he may have changed much sooner without her push.

4. *Rebellion*

Not only do women's efforts fail to change a man, but they often bring out a rebellious streak in him. This is caused by his struggle to maintain his freedom.

I have a son who occasionally says, "Mother, don't tell me to do it or I won't want to." This indicates how men feel at heart. They, in fact, sometimes turn against the very thing which they want—because of their rebellious natures.

An Impressive Illustration—*Rebellion*

A woman became converted to a particular religion and was very devoted to it. She tried to interest her husband, but he did not respond. She kept after him day and night, but each effort was fruitless.

One evening she arranged secretly for the missionaries of her church to drop by at dinnertime. She felt that her husband would feel obligated to invite them in and be friendly. She also arranged that they have with them materials from which they could preach to him after the meal.

Everything went exactly as planned, for just as they were sitting down to the table the missionaries rang the doorbell. After an enjoyable, friendly meal the wife said, "Wouldn't it be nice if we had these two gentlemen explain a little about the church?" Due to moral pressure and courtesy he agreed.

As the missionaries were assembling their materials, flannel board, books and pictures, the poor man felt trapped. He excused himself to go to the bathroom, climbed out the bathroom window and disappeared. He was gone for three days.

After three days of searching, the desperate wife turned to her church for help. Several of the leaders came to her rescue and started looking for him. After an extensive search he was found. In questioning him it was discovered that he had no intention of returning to his home at all. However, due to the kindly persuasion of the gentleman that found him, and his wife's promises that she would never mention religion again, he returned to his home. The wife kept her promise "to the letter," and the man began to relax in peace.

The impressive part of this story is the following experience: The gentleman who found him became quite well acquainted with the husband, who confessed, "I don't have anything against your church. In fact, I have for some time wanted to know more about it, but not from my wife."

Secretly he learned more about his wife's religion, became converted to it and secretly became a member of it. Then one morning in church the bishop arose and announced that there was a new member of his congregation, gave his name, and asked him to come to the rostrum. The wife was so overjoyed that she burst into tears.

Another Illustration of Rebellion

Another woman caused a rebellious streak to appear in her husband. When she first married him she made many suggestions about trivial matters. She tried to reform his eating habits, encouraged him to take more baths, and to take them more thoroughly, and to take better care of his appearance. She had been taught the importance of nutrition, but her husband came from a family that thought it unimportant. It was especially irritating to him to be deprived of certain foods which he had been used to.

This infringement upon his freedom caused him to eat especially unwholesome foods while away from home, and he began drinking. Her suggestions were towards health, so his rebellion was against health. In a sense it was *"Give me liberty or give me death."*

She has not been successful in changing him, and he has continued his rebellious habits to this day. Not all men react so violently against suggestions, but even the more sensible ones are resentful towards the women who try to change them.

As you can see from the four problems that I have just illustrated, *women's efforts to change men are invariably unsuccessful* in that they lead to marriage problems, tend to destroy love, do not bring any change in the man, and can even lead to his rebellion.

The Plan that Works

There is a plan whereby a man can change and it is called freedom. It is not 100 percent sure, but it is the only possible way a man can grow. It is the only effective plan and the only way to man's happiness. It is also the only setting for love to flourish.

Free agency is one of the most fundamental laws of life. Mankind does not develop nor is he happy without it. The Lord was fully aware of this eternal principle when he created man and placed him on the earth. He allowed the forces of evil to be present, although he knew from the beginning that many of the precious souls of men would fall into sin and reap the bitterness that comes from disobedience. But he also knew that without freedom mankind cannot develop. Man has to be given a choice and has to make that choice himself.

If the Lord could risk man's future happiness and well being in order to extend to him his precious freedom, why then cannot women allow men the same privilege? Why not let him do the things he wants to do, be the kind of man he wants to be without interference?

"But," you might say, "in my efforts to improve my husband I do not take away his freedom, for I never insist on anything nor do I use any element of force." But it is not by compulsion, but in the more subtle ways that we interfere. It is by the following that we take away a man's freedom:

How We Take Away Man's Freedom

1. Moral Pressure
3. Disapproval
3. Suggestions
4. Hinting
5. Pushing, Nagging
6. Open Criticism

Every man wants to live in peace. Every man wants approval. When you use moral pressure you make him choose between his freedom and "peace in the household."

Sometimes he chooses peace and sacrifices his freedom. For example, a young couple who were guests in my home planned a day at the beach. As they were leaving, the girl asked her husband, "Aren't you going to wear your dark glasses?" He told her that he deliberately left them for he didn't want to be bothered. She tried to insist, but he held his ground. After they were in the car I heard the car door open and the man came back for his glasses. All he said was, "Anything to keep peace!"

There are times when a man will give up his precious freedom temporarily because his wife makes it so tough for him that he has no alternative. But not always will he sacrifice freedom for peace. Many times a man will cling devotedly to his freedom at all costs.

A young wife told me that each Sunday morning she merely asked her husband, "Are you planning to attend church this morning?" Although he wanted to please his wife, this gentle hint so irritated him that he stayed home just to hold to his freedom. He had nothing against church, but if he attended, he wanted it to be his idea. As soon as she stopped hinting, he began attending more regularly.

Religious freedom is precious. Our very nation was founded on the principle of religious liberty. The pilgrims left Europe to obtain this precious freedom. When we attempt to drive men to church we more often drive them away. Not only is pushing unsuccessful, but it is *unrighteous.*

The few women who have successfully pushed their husbands into church activity take credit for it under false illusions. Their men would have come into activity much sooner with freedom, appreciation, and a shining example. Such men have found some other reason for attendance at church than the woman realizes.

PROVOKE A MAN TO RIGHTEOUSNESS

There are some Christian Women who have been taught "to provoke their husbands to righteousness." But the word provoke does not mean what is commonly implied. The true meaning of the word is to incite, to inspire, or to arouse. *It does not mean to nettle or to push.*

WOMEN ARE SELF RIGHTEOUS

Why do women try to change men? Because they have a self righteous attitude. They feel that they put forth more effort into doing what is right, try more diligently to make marriage successful, are more active in church, and are better persons than are their husbands. They look down on men, and therefore feel that the men, not themselves, need to improve.

The Sadducees and the Pharisees in Biblical times had this same self-righteous attitude. They were faithful to attend church, paid tithes, prayed, read the scriptures, fasted, observed any number of rituals, but the Savior called them "hypocrites", not because of their faithfulness, but because of their self-righteousness.

Woman is in no position to judge a man's worth. Can you set yourself up as a judge? Are you in reality better than he?

A girl confessed to me many serious faults which her husband had, then I said: "Do you really think that you are better then he is?" At first she looked at me with indignation. Then, after quiet meditation, she bowed her head and said humbly, "No, I don't think I am a better person than my husband. I know he is a fine man at heart."

The Christian Attitude

The very heart of Christian doctrine is: *It is ourselves we must change.* We have been told to cast out the beam from our own eye first, and then we will more clearly see the mote which is in our brother's. Women who try to change their men trample on their freedom, and violate righteous principles.

Will He Change?

You might wonder, "If I accept him at face value, is there any hope that he himself might make some effort to improve?" Who is to say? You must accept the fact that he may not. But in a mysterious way men are very apt to improve when they are fully accepted and given their freedom.

The only hope that a man will change is for you to not try to change him. Others may try to change him, teach him, and offer suggestions, but the woman he loves must accept him for the man he is.

If men get to heaven they want it to be their idea. If they go to church they want it to be their idea. If they make improvement in their character, their health, their personality, or their business, they want it to be from their own initiative. And when given such freedom, *they are very apt to change for the better.* Let me illustrate:

A Success Story (Freedom)

You will remember the girl who tried to change her

husband's eating habits. Another girl of my aquaintance used an opposite approach—one of complete freedom.

She also came from a family with strict eating habits, but she extended complete freedom to her husband. Soon after they were married she said sweetly to him, "Now, honey, I know that I have been trained to eat a different way than you, but do you mind if I prepare for myself the foods I want, and I will do the same for you." He agreed, and she did this for many months. But after awhile he adopted her good eating habits and was preaching their value to others. Men are usually sensible. They want what is right and best for them, but more than anything else they want their precious freedom.

A SUCCESS STORY (FREEDOM)

A woman was engaged to marry a man of a different religion than her own. Her religion was very important to her, and she hoped that if she married him he would eventually join her church.

She sought counsel from a very wise man who told her, "If you do marry this man make nothing of his religious differences to him openly. Do not attempt to change his views. If he wants to go to his church, go with him. Give him complete freedom but hold to your ideals and be the living example of what your religion teaches."

She did marry the man, and she followed the wise man's advice. He did ask her to attend his church with him which she did willingly. In return he was willing to attend hers. By comparing the two he soon became convinced that his wife's church was superior to his own, and he became a member of it.

In your attempt to accept your man at face value many problems may come your way. What do you do when his faults continue to irritate you and you find them difficult to overlook? What do you do when he does something ignoble, far below your standards? In accepting him must you also give up any of your own ideals or virtues? What do you do if he mistreats you—must you also accept this? All of these questions I will answer one by one.

LOOK TO HIS BETTER SIDE

Once you come to accept a man at face value you can stop

worrying about his faults. This is made easy if you will *look to his better side* and concentrate on that. For years you may have been so concerned about improving him that you have overlooked his virtues. Most men are Dr. Jeckyl and Mr. Hydes, and, it is only by recognizing and continually believing in their better side that you can help a man, a child, or any individual to grow.

Try to imagine that your husband is painted partly bright and partly dull. Then turn the dull side out of view so that only the bright shows. You know the dull is there, but you are not looking at it. You see only the bright. Then tell him that you appreciate his better side. And be specific!

It will help your discovery of his better side if you understand that there are virtues behind many of men's faults. For example, an obnoxious man is often a true sign of a high caliber man that is not appreciated, not accepted, not given his freedom, or in some way mistreated by his wife. A man who is moody and discouraged is often a man with extremely high aspirations that are not being met. A man who is forgetful, negligent, thoughtless, is often a man who has great mental capacity, and is using his mind for greater things than what appear to be important details to you. A man who appears lazy and negligent at home may very well be a man who is putting all his energies towards making his life away from home a success and becoming a good provider.

What to Do When He Does Something Wrong

If your husband is at times dishonest, unkind, weak, or shows lack of character, you may wonder just how to react. You accept him at face value, but if you completely overlook an evil act it displays a weakness in your own character.

The thing to do is to first show reluctance to believe it. Say that you thought it was not possible for a man such as he to do such a thing. If you are compelled to believe it, indicate that you know it is contrary to his true nature, and was only the result of carelessness or thoughtlessness. *You must be immensely disappointed at his temporary lapse, but your faith in his better side must be unshaken.*

When He Mistreats You

Must you accept a man at face value when he mistreats you and just overlook it? I am referring to times when he may be thoughtless, unfair, impose on you, neglect you too far, or is extremely harsh or critical. Man is entitled to many freedoms, but he does not have the right to mistreat you. You are a human being, worthy of respect and consideration and it is important to both of you that you maintain your self dignity. In fact, it is difficult for a man to feel kindly towards a woman whom he can mistreat.

One of the high rewards which comes from living the whole of Fascinating Womanhood is consideration and respect from one's husband. However, one need not wait until such a high goal is achieved to command respect and proper treatment. Knowing how to handle these difficult situations is one of the charming arts of Fascinating Womanhood and will be taught in chapter 18.

Hold to Your Own Ideals

The question may arise—In accepting a man at face value, should I ever lower my own standards to meet his and thereby make him feel more accepted. The answer is no. He will not respect you for it. A man likes to consider woman as finer, better and holier than himself, and therefore, it would be a disappointment to him to see you fall from your level onto his. You owe it to yourself and the development of your Angelic side to always maintain as high a standard as possible.

The question may also arise—Is there ever a time when you should try to change a man? *No!* He must be accepted at face value. But, there is a time, as I briefly mentioned before, when you should try to open his eyes to his own mistakes, but only in a particular situation.

When a Man Is Blind to His Own Mistakes

Often a man is blind to his own mistakes and such blindness causes him to get into difficulty with his associates or fail to reach success. On these occasions his wife should open his eyes.

Take for example, the salesman who uses a poor approach, or the department supervisor who is too dictatorial to his fellow employees, or the doctor who is losing patients because he appears unfriendly, or even the man who is shunned because he has body odors.

On these occasions his wife should alert him. He will not resent it if done in the right way. Often others who observe his mistakes are not interested enough to awaken him, or may feel it not their business to do so. His wife may be the only one who cares enough about him to help.

The Proper Approach: Keep in mind that *you do accept him*. It is the world that does not! Others are offended, not you. Tell him you have a few ideas which might prove helpful. Let him know that you are not close to the situation as he is and that you could be wrong, but "could this be the cause of his trouble?" Assure him that you admire him and isn't it regrettable that others do not appreciate him for his true worth.

Once you have opened his eyes, do not persist in the matter. Drop it completely. If he continues to make mistakes, fully aware of them, you must allow him this freedom.

Be certain that he is actually unaware of his mistakes and also be certain that it is causing him difficulty. A woman asked me if she should correct her husband's grammar which was obviously poor. In inquiring about him I found that he was extremely successful and had approval of many friends. I told her that I felt it unnecessary to say anything about it.

When you give your opinions or corrections to your husband, be feminine. Don't appear to know more about his business than he does; don't be motherly, and don't talk man to man. (Refer to Chapter 7—How to Give Feminine Advice.)

SUMMARY

We have learned the importance of acceptance, and that if we try to change a man we are doomed to fail—this will create marriage problems, and may cause a man to rebel. We have also learned that it is difficult, if not impossible, for a man to love the woman who pushes him, corrects him, or tries to improve him. We know now that we are in no position to judge a man's worth and that we tend to do this because of our self righteous attitudes. It is ourselves we need to change—not our husbands. We must look to his better side. And if we want to become Angela Human and win his Celestial Love, *we must accept him at face value.*

Some to whom I have taught this philosophy say that it is difficult to accept a man, and therefore have stopped trying. Admittedly, acceptance is not easy to live, but it is based upon a principle of Christianity, and one might as well stop trying to become a Christian as to stop accepting a man at face value.

There are several steps to acceptance, or rules to observe. They are:

STEPS TO ACCEPTANCE

1. *Get Rid of Your Self Righteous Attitude.* Approach this from a religious standpoint, realizing that a self-righteous attitude is a serious sin and shows lack of humility and therefore lack of character. Remember the Bible account of the man who lifted his head in pride, saying that he was glad he was not sinful as other men, but Jesus approved the humble man who smote his chest saying, "Oh, God, be merciful to me, a sinner."

2. *Look to His Better Side.* Acceptance is made easier if you concentrate on his virtues, and develop an appreciation of his better side, and tell him of your appreciation. In this way he will grow, and his faults will soon cease to annoy you.

3. *Don't Use Other Men as Shining Examples.* Women often use a brother, father, an outstanding man of the community, or even her own son as a shining example of manhood, thinking that by so doing her husband will try to copy the other man's virtues. This is a demonstration of the woman's efforts to change her husband and must be eliminated if a man is to feel accepted. The blow to his ego is an even more serious effect.

4. *Tell Him that You Accept Him.* It is difficult for some women to "break the ice." I have given some practical assignments at the end of this chapter of just what to say to him if you are in doubt. It is not enough to merely think about it. You must tell him.

OUR REWARD

What reward can we expect for all of our efforts? I can promise you that it is love that you will receive in return. *When you cast your bread upon the waters, it comes back buttered.* Love is the central message of this book, and I have stated in the beginning that a woman has the power to arouse a man's feelings towards her. Acceptance is the first, most vital step towards this goal.

When you truly accept a man you awaken some of his deepest sentiments towards you. And when you give a man his freedom, allow him to be the kind of man he wants to be, you gain a strange power over him. It is a part of the Power of Fascinating Womanhood.

And when you accept him, you will cease being concerned about his faults, and will therefore be able to see more clearly his virtues. You will appreciate him more, love him more, and he will offer you love, tenderness and other kindnesses you had not thought possible, as in the following true experiences:

Success Story

A girl had a darling husband, but he had some habits she disapproved of, especially his use of tobacco. She insisted he go into their cellar to smoke even though she had accepted this in him when they were married.

After learning the philosophy of Fascinating Womanhood she realized how awful she had been. When he came home that night she confessed her feelings, asking for forgiveness for the terrible way she had treated him, and told him that she accepted him as he was. The man was so tenderly touched that he cried. Later that evening he told her that he loved her for the first time in two years and he slept with his arm around her all night.

Success Story

"My husband has been quite a fellow to go out with the boys, almost every night until dawn. Each time I have been extremely aggravated with him. After understanding the principle of acceptance, however, I have tried a different approach.

"One night I had dinner on the table and had called him to eat when one of his buddies came to the door, wanting him to go out for awhile. He got his coat on and told me where he was going and not to wait up for him. Although my first impulse was to hit the ceiling, I caught myself and said, instead, 'Oh, I think that's a good idea! You really need to get away for awhile. Have a good time and I'll have something for you to eat when you come home.'

"His reaction was one of great surprise, as it was to his friend. He did go, but in about 45 minutes he was back home in very happy spirits, with a box of candy for me. He spent the rest of the evening just talking with me and helping me."

SUCCESS STORY

A married girl who had been trampling on her husband's religious freedom had the following to tell: When she realized her mistakes, she said to him, "You are the most important thing in life to me. I want you to be happy. I realize how wrong I have been to try to push you into church activity."

The man got a peculiar look on his face—something happened within him. He said, "If you are this fair with me I will be equally fair with you. Before, I have thought I would like you to give up your church activity, but now I want you to have the freedom to continue."

SUCCESS STORY

Another case was that of a woman who had already visited a lawyer seeking divorce, but when taught this doctrine she determined to give her marriage another try. The first words she said to her husband were:

"May I have some of your precious time. I would like to ask forgiveness for not understanding you all this time. Will you allow me the privilege of showing you that I have learned the importance of understanding you. I want you to know how wrong I've been about you all these years."

"I am happy that you are the kind of man you are, and that you are not like putty in my hands and have had the courage of your convictions all these years."

A very strange look appeared on his face, and she could detect that something was happening inside him.She went to her work in a beauty shop, but about midday, her husband, who had previously been indifferent, spiteful and negligent, called her on the phone and said, "I hate to think of you on this miserable day [rainy] working so hard. Why don't you close up shop and come home." She did, and when she arrived he had a dinner date planned for the two of them.

The following day she was leaving the house and he noticed a run in her hose. She told him it was the last pair she had, to which he said, "I'll see to it that you have a supply." The following day he bought her six pair.

He also bought her a new bed, although they had not been sleeping together. And I was informed that they are now sleeping together.

A few days later, this man who had never been helpful or accommodating, was down to his wife's shop fixing her hair dryers.

And this is similar to the success you will feel if you accept your man at face value. The men in these cases read no books nor took any classes about how to treat a woman. *The woman aroused his feelings and his actions herself.* It isn't necessary for the man to know anything about this subject. You can win his heart and devotion by the way you treat him.

YOUR ASSIGNMENT (AN ICE BREAKER)

The following is an illustration of what you might say to your husband to let him know you accept him.

"I am happy that you are the kind of man you are. I can see that I have not understood you in the past, and that I have made many mistakes."

"I am glad that you have not allowed me to push you around, and have not been like putty in my hands, but have had the courage of your convictions."

"Will you forgive me, and let me prove to you how happy I am that you are just as you are."

At first, you may feel insincere by telling him these things, for all of your critical attitudes may not have disappeared. But do tell him, regardless, and look to his better side. If you continue to express yourself it will help you to grow towards full acceptance.

Remember to observe all four of the steps to acceptance:
1. Get rid of your self-righteous attitude.
2. Look to his better side.
3. Do not use other men as shining examples.
4. Express your acceptance.

CHAPTER IV

Admiration

The center of woman's happiness in marriage is to be loved by her mate—but the center of man's is to be admired.

Deep in his heart every man longs for admiration—of his abilities, his ideas, and his dreams. This admiration is his greatest happiness, and the lack of it one of his most distressing miseries. Although it is all important to him, it isn't something which he can get for himself. It must be given him by those who respect and love him. He likes receiving it from any and every source, but it is most essential from the woman he loves.

A man will often do and say things deliberately in the presence of a woman, hoping to receive admiration. But these things will often go unnoticed. Usually a woman is too busy, or too mentally occupied with her own world and problems to notice anything to admire. Women don't often bother to find out what is in a man's heart, what he thinks about and dreams about. But the woman who offers the perfect admiration is the woman who wins his heart and soul.

THE YOUNG BOY

This need is manifest in the young boy, and is essential to his confidence and growth into manhood. It helps him to experience love for his parents. But, unfortunately, there are many young boys whose parents fail to admire them. A life of correction without praise some young men endure, but the longing is always there.

When such a boy matures, he needs admiration more than ever, for doing without it in his youth has caused a lack of confidence. If the woman he marries can offer the needed admiration his troubles are over. If not, he often becomes a lonely creature.

THE YOUNG MARRIED MAN

Especially is the need for admiration apparent in the young married man just beginning his career. He expects to be an all-conquering success; no project is too wild, no dream too fantastic. He is full of plans and proposals, assurance and enthusiasm. What he doesn't expect to do, after a little preliminary preparation, of course, simply isn't worth doing. He can find a hundred flaws in the way older heads are managing things now—but you just wait until he gets his chance and revolutionizes matters. Meantime, life isn't worth living if he can't find someone to whom he can tell all this, how things ought to be, how they will be when he gets his chance.

Most of his youthful associates are too much occupied with their own aspirations to listen to his. Older people will only laugh at him. Where can he find an uncritical listener and confidante? *The cry of his soul is for admiration.* The woman who gives it to him is no less than an angel.

THE OLDER MAN

As a man grows older, if he has not been admired, he often learns to do without it. He becomes, it would seem, hardened, incredulous, and less sensitive to the lack of admiration. The older a man becomes, however, the more bitterly he resents this apparent indifference to the bigger and nobler elements of his character. He represses his craving for admiration because he does not believe it is to be had, but the craving for it is just as strong and persistent as it is in the younger man.

WHAT HE WANTS YOU TO ADMIRE

What a man wants you to admire more than anything else are *his manly qualities.* If you admire the qualities which are admirable in both men and women he will be disappointed. For example, if he helps you with the dishes is kind and thoughtful, is tidy, well-groomed and has good taste—these virtues are worthy of some praise—but this is not the type of admiration that will stir him inside. It is his masculinity that he wants noticed and admired.

Admire:

1. His superior strength
2. His manly courage

3. His sense of honor and duty in men's affairs
4. His leadership ability
5. His sexual capacities
6. His determination and power
7. His devotion to a cause
8. His mental capacity
9. His unyielding steadfastness
10. How clever are his tactics in the world of men
11. His achievement, success, or excellence
12. How decisive his judgement and decisions
13. How noble are his masculine ideals, standards and aspirations

These are the things a man longs for, *for they make him feel like a real man.* And it is this realization of his masculinity that stirs his soul, and arouses his sentiment towards the woman who has made him feel this way.

It may be difficult for you to find such outstanding traits of character in your mate from day to day. But there are many common evidences of manliness which we can observe very frequently.

THE MORE COMMON MANLY CHARACTERISTICS

1. The hours he spends at work to provide you with the necessities.
2. His strength in: mowing the lawn, moving heavy objects, painting, opening tight jar lids, turning screws, or wielding a hammer.
3. The manner in which he rules over you and his children.
4. His beard, his mustache (women don't have them—they are strictly masculine.)
5. Skill in repairing a motor.
6. His body structure.
7. His sex response.
8. His stubbornness (common term for determination).
9. His heavy gait.
10. The masculine clothes he wears (tell him that you admire manly clothes).
11. His deep pitched voice.
12. His heavy jaw, or large shoulders.
13. His masculine hands—their size—their strength.
14. His dependability in his work, other manly responsibilities.

How to Develop Admiration

If you have not already admired your husband adequately you will be interested in the following suggestions:

1. *Set out to discover him.* There may be many things about him which for years you have overlooked. He will undoubtedly have some manly qualities worthy of your admiration. He will have either intellectual gifts, physical brawn, or masculine skill.

2. *Become interested in him.* If you will spend less time thinking about your affairs and your problems and more in thinking about him, you will find many qualities which before went unnoticed. Women tend to become self-centered. Our lives are wrapped up in our children and our household chores. But it is such self-centeredness and lack of interest that causes a man to turn to a more appreciative woman.

3. *Listen to him talk.* This is a wonderful way to discover him. Few women know much about their husband's activities away from home, and they are therefore not aware of their men's accomplishments and special abilities. The only opportunity they have to know about them, as a rule, is to listen to them talk.

If a man has a good listener he will enjoy telling of his life away from home. Take every opportunity to listen to him. Often he talks for the sole purpose of gaining your admiration. Imagine how disappointing it is to be turned away empty—by your lack of interest.

But it is important that you learn *how* to listen to a man.

How to Listen to a Man

Follow this rule, and you can learn to be a good listener: *Do not listen only to what he is saying, but to the man who is saying it.* Notice how absorbed he is in the subject, how he has mastered the intricate details, how he glories in his skill and knowledge, how he has worked out and developed his own ideas, how loyal and devoted he is to them, what mental and moral power he can wield, what a genuine man he is when you stop and appreciate him.

If you can't comprehend all of what he is saying, look for the traits of his character which you can admire. His conversation will reveal them. In fact, if you only follow his subject, and appreciate that, and not the man who is thus expressing himself, he will be disappointed. You may rest assured that he is not talking only to have his subject appreciated. He wants admiration to be bestowed upon himself as a man and not as a mere talking machine.

A woman need not be well educated, or possess high intelligence to follow a clever man's discourse. In his pleasure at having himself admired the man seldom notices that his conversation is not understood. Even when he does notice it he relishes it, as in the following words:

> What care I though she appear not to understand?
> Do you think it is for a sublime word I thirst
> When I feel that a soul is gazing into my soul?
> —Maeterlinck

If you learn to listen to a man correctly it doesn't matter if the subject is interesting or dull. You may converse on world affairs, the atom bomb, or the intricate details of his business career, and you will be able to maintain an interest. In fact, you can safely guess that if he deliberately talks over your head he is doing so only to arouse your admiration. The following story will illustrate the correct way to listen.

THE RIGHT WAY TO LISTEN

Jim is a man who craves admiration, for out in the world he gets little of it. He is a terrific success in business circles, is highly intellectual, and has ingenious political ideas, but who cares, or bothers to find out about them? In fact, some have implied that only luck is responsible for his success.

But at home it is a different story. His wife knows little about politics, but she does admire Jim.

No sooner do they have a few minutes together than she steers the conversation into the channel of politics. She prods him from time to time until he is thoroughly wound up in his hobby, and then she listens. If you will observe her carefully you will find that she listens only casually to what he says, but that she nevertheless finds a great deal to admire. What on earth is it? Not his appearance, because he is just an average looking man; not his language, for hers is just as good as his; and not his ideas, for they are of little interest to her.

She sees loyalty and courage and idealism. Here is a man

whose heart rings true to his ideals, to what he believes fair and square. Whether she agrees with him or not doesn't matter. So she sits there and admires, not his words, not his ideas, but his *manliness*. His fervent enthusiasm which might irritate others who do not agree with him is regarded by her as another expression of the glorious and steadfast champion that he is.

So long as she can watch the rapt animation of his countenance and the unfolding of his admirable character she asks nothing else.

Even his moods of depression arouse admiration in her. Isn't he depressed only because of what he considers the futility of many of his ideas?

WHAT IF YOU FAIL TO FIND ANY MANLY QUALITIES IN HIM?

In extreme cases a man may deteriorate to the point that he is really not much of a man—on the surface. What can you do if you cannot find anything to admire?

1. *Have faith* that these qualities exist in him even though they may not be showing.

These qualities do exist, in dormant form within his soul, as they do in the souls of all men. Having faith in their existence and believing that there is the possibility of his becoming a real man is only another way of giving him an ideal to live up to, or using the power of positive thinking.

Goethe, the German author said: "If you treat a man as he is, he will stay as he is, but if you treat him as if he were what he ought to be, and could be, he will become that bigger and better man."

The woman who has an unwavering faith in a man's better side although it may not be showing inspires a man to live up to such a conception of his ability. She offers him hope that perhaps he hasn't appreciated himself at his true value—that courage, steadfastness, and nobility really are the underlying traits of his character.

Many a girl has transformed a man from an apparently stupid, weak, lazy, cowardly, unrighteous man into a determined, energetic, true and noble one.

Often a man is at heart a stout-hearted creature and only needs someone to suggest to him that his life does not do justice to his true character. Once persuaded that he is noble at heart, and that you perceive it, he becomes anxious to show both to himself and you that there is no mistake about the matter. The turning point of many a man's life comes from just such a revelation of his higher capabilities.

In this way, and only in this way, does a woman bring out *the best in her man*—by her unwavering belief in his better side. It is the only encouragement he needs. A woman should not encourage her man by pushing but by her belief in his better side.

2. *Go back into the past.* If you cannot find anything manly to appreciate in the present, you can dwell on past observations. Be specific, and bring up instances which aroused your admiration. Even though it is in the past it will stir his heart.

One of my students said that she found it necessary to think back to the days of the depression. She remembered those trying years when steady employment was difficult to find. And she could recall how her husband walked the shoe leather from the soles of his shoes in his persistent effort to provide for his family. It was only through his diligence and determination that his family continued to enjoy the comforts of life.

Since that time, their marriage had deteriorated, and he had become a difficult man to live with. But when she expressed her admiration, even though it was in the distant past, her husband melted, and she could detect that at that moment a change took place within his soul—and he began to develop a new attitude towards her. Since then their marriage has blossomed once again.

How to Express Admiration

One of my students said that after hearing my instructions about admiration she said to her husband, "My, you're a manly sort of man." And he asked, "How? In just what way do you mean?" She couldn't think of any particular occasions and was very embarrassed.

1. *Be specific.* It is better if you don't talk in generalities. Think of specific instances when his masculinity is or was noticeable.

If you can't think of any, try to word it so he cannot "pin you down to specifics." Say, for example: "I am glad I married a strong, dominant man!" Or "You take such good care of me." Or "You provide for me so well."

2. *The way to say it.* Speak with warmth and tenderness and with admiration radiating from your eyes.

You Must Accept Him

I must warn you that the most important step to understanding man and winning his heart is accepting him at face value. Your admiration of him will fail to be effective if you still hold in your heart critical attitudes, take away his freedom, or try to change him.

If you admire him in some ways but are critical of him in others—if you do not accept him at face value, it will be like serving him a piece of moldy pie and trying to disguise it by putting whipped cream on top. Your admiration will be detected as insincere and will be ineffective.

Summary

I have told you that the cry of man's soul is for admiration of his masculine abilities and achievements. I have also told you that you can develop the art of admiration by setting out to discover him, becoming interested in all that he does, and by listening to him talk. I have also told you to be specific in expressing yourself as often as possible, and to speak with warmth and tenderness. And finally, I have said that you must have an underlying attitude of acceptance.

Rewards

It may seem that you are doing a great amount of giving, and what are you to receive from all this? The rewards for your efforts will be tremendous, and I can promise you that you will gain a strange but righteous power over your man.

Although his love might have been asleep for some time, it will awaken, and he will shower you with loving endearment. And if he has already been loving you he will do so with even more sincerity, with almost reverance. One woman told me that her husband began kissing her feet when she began treating him like a man.

Many women experience within a few weeks a more fulfilling sex life—a greater sex response within the man, as well as in the woman.

Another benefit is that it will make acceptance fairly easy. Once you begin searching for his traits of character and concentrate on the better side of him, the faults that you might formerly have dwelt on become insignificant. You begin to appreciate him more and love him more.

But perhaps the most noticable result is that it so definitely defines the difference between man and woman. When you become aware of your husband's masculinity you become aware of the many differences between the sexes. You become aware of your womanliness which is a thrilling sensation. This makes you feel like a woman and causes him to treat you with respect due the feminine sex. *If you treat him like a man he will treat you like a woman.*

These are only the basic rewards that will come to you. Other things he may shower on you may come to you as a surprise as in some of the success stories which follow:

SUCCESS STORY

One of the most dramatic cases of my experience was of a young couple who were on the brink of divorce—due to the husband's insistence. They had many problems, and he had some major faults. He had never bought his wife anything, although he had money in savings for himself for a trip to Japan; he resented his baby and said, "She stands in the way of my success." He withheld marital love, grudgingly. He allowed his wife to work, although she didn't want to—while he planned an expensive trip to Japan. He was losing his faith in God, and he didn't want any more children.

But his wife didn't want a divorce and came to my classes of instruction. After hearing the lesson on manliness she decided to try admiring him. He is a handsome man, 6′4′′, with an especially well built body. But all she said to him was: "I have always admired your manly strength—your beautiful muscles."

She said that something took place within his soul. She couldn't explain it exactly but it was a peculiar look on his face. He didn't say anything in response but was very quiet. And if I remember correctly, I think she said he started singing quietly.

Within a few days, he took the money he had saved for Japan and bought her household furniture. Within a few weeks, although marital love had been withheld, he now offered it willingly. He has returned to his religion and is joyfully anticipating the birth of a new baby.

I know this story sounds too dramatic to be true, but it is nevertheless true and happened just as I told it. Of course this girl continued to look for traits to admire in him. But she believes that his awakening was when she first complimented his muscular strength.

SUCCESS STORY

This should not be termed a success story, but it does illustrate the power of admiration.

A young man whom I know cannot seem to find his niche in life. He really wants to be a policeman, but he cannot, for he always fails the eye test. No one has been able to rid him of this burning desire.

In talking to his wife the truth came to light. When they were dating she expressed glowing admiration for policemen and was occasionally almost gushing. She would say to him, "Oh, look, look, don't they look handsome in their uniforms!" and "They look so brave and so strong," and "I'll bet they're not afraid of anything." Is it any wonder that he would like to copy them and have such admiration bestowed upon himself?

SUCCESS STORY

A woman whose husband had been treating her with indifference admired her husband's honesty by saying, "You're as honest as Abe Lincoln." A previous antagonism left immediately, and within a few days he could not remember having felt anything but kindly. And he said to her, tenderly, "The best part of all this is that it gets better as you get older."

Another woman told me that in all her married years her husband had never treated her "decent" until she began admiring his masculinity.

Another said that all she did was admire the way her husband was building a motor car for his son, and he helped her with the dishes for the first time in 25 years.

It may be difficult for some to "break the ice," but do take the initiative to say something. The following suggestions might help:

Assignment

Tell him:

1. "I appreciate the fact that you work and slave to provide necessities and comforts for your little ones."

2. If he is fixing the car: "It must be terribly complicated to repair something as intricate as the interior of a motor car."

3. If he is painting the fence: "You paint with little effort. I'm afraid it would be very tiring to me."

4. "I am happy that you are a man who has the courage of his convictions." (whatever they might be.)

5. "I admire the manly courage you have in solving your difficult problems."

6. When he is dreaming: "I am happy that I married a man with some rainbows—some masculine aspirations."

7. "To have a man to rule over me makes me feel like a woman."

In addition, you must listen to his conversation and admire the manly that you see there also.

Remember: *You cannot become Angela Human and arouse a man's Celestial Love if you do not make him feel like a man.*

CHAPTER V

A Man's Pride

And of what is man proud? *He is proud of his manly qualities* of which I spoke in the previous chapter. He likes to show them off, to call your attention to them in both conversation and actions. Like every male creature from the peacock and the rooster, to the bull and the lion, he likes to strut before the female of the species and show what manly powers are his. He likes to enjoy the admiration which these traits arouse.

But it is here man is most vulnerable, for his pride is extremely sensitive. He cannot bear to have his masculinity *belittled, ridiculed, or treated with indifference.*

Let us review again these masculine traits:

1. Physically: It is his strength, his body structure, and his sexual abilities.
2. Spiritually: It is his courage, honor, determination, aspirations and ideals.
3. Mentally: It is his cleverness, intellectual gifts, achievements, leadership, skills.

WHAT HE SUFFERS

When a man is belittled it is humiliation he suffers. It can be a sharp-bladed cutting sensation, or a crushing feeling. Whatever the forms of humiliation, it is a painful experience.

SERIOUS EFFECTS OF INJURED PRIDE

If it were only the cutting and crushing sensations of humiliation which man suffers he could probably bear it. But there are more detrimental effects which we must understand.

RESERVE

1. *Reserve:* When a man is belittled frequently he tends to build a tight wall of reserve around himself—an impenetrable barrier against those who have offended him.

When this occurs he appears distant. He may talk but does

so cautiously. You cannot tell his innermost feelings, for he doesn't expose them. He will not confide although you may sense his longing to do so. He is reserved in his actions. He tells little of his accomplishments, problems or dreams. Through all of this you can detect an unhappy feeling in him.

Occasionally a man will clam up and not talk at all. This is called going into his shell. It is as though he has climbed inside himself, locked the door and pulled down the blinds. It is difficult and seemingly impossible to get next to him.

This tendency for a man to build a wall of reserve is common. The finer the caliber of the man the more he tends to draw into himself when his pride is hurt.

WHAT IS THE MATTER WITH HIM?

It is most important that you understand what he suffers. First, he is proud. He would love to strut around as the bull and lion and have you admire his dreams, hopes, achievements, and skills—all of the admirable traits which he has locked inside himself. But he cannot. He dare not! Why? Because he is afraid of further contempt or indifference. He will not expose his precious ideas to you because of this fear. He longs to confide—to pour out his heart to you, but fear blocks his way—the fear of further humiliation. These two conflicting feelings seem to be fighting inside him—*the desire to be admired*—versus *the fear of humiliation*. And this conflict is what makes him so miserable.

There should be no barrier of reserve between husband and wife in the ideal marriage—which is the theme of this philosophy. A man should always be able to express himself in words or actions without fear. When he has a desire to pour out his heart he should feel no barrier. If you can sense this reserve in your husband you should take steps to break it down. If you do not eliminate it, he may be driven to another in whom he can confide.

HOW TO BREAK DOWN THE WALL OF RESERVE

You cannot attempt to pull him out of his shell. You must break his wall of reserve down indirectly—secretly, by the following procedure:

1. You must accept him. If you continue your criticism or

dissatisfaction of him, he will not feel like exposing his innermost feelings to your unappreciative attitude.

2. Admire his masculinity. Your admiration will do more to break down his reserve than any effort you can make.

3. Cease belittling him. You will have to eliminate any remarks which crush his male ego.

4. Don't be critical of others. If you are a backbiting fault-finding woman he will never trust his precious thoughts to you.

5. Hold confidences sacred. You must prove that you will not repeat to others the things he confides to you. Even though *you* admire him, how does he know others will? They might ridicule the things which you admire. He doesn't want their contempt or indifference either.

Remember: *Nothing but the absolute certainty that he will not be met with further ridicule or indifference will induce him to lay down his armor of reserve.*

It is important that you know how to treat a man when he is withdrawn. You cannot pull him out directly, as I have stated. Nor should you make him feel ashamed of his peculiar behavior by saying, "Why are you so quiet?" or "I can't see why you don't ever tell me anything." Nor can you pry into him and try to see if you can tell what is the matter.

The only acceptable way to treat him is to be tender and reassuring. If you will pat his cheek and tell him how proud you are of him he might melt on the spot. This is the only thing you can do at the moment and the only comfort he needs.

I have said that reserve is one serious effect of man's injured pride. But as long as a man has a reserve, at least it is a healthy sign of his sensitivity. The following result of injured pride is far more serious.

2. *The Numbing Effect*: When a man's pride is injured over a long period of time he learns to protect himself from the hurt by hardening himself against it. He learns not to care. His senses become dulled, or numb.

In Dr. Edrita Fried's book, *The Ego in Love and Sexuality*, she speaks of this numbing effect. But Dr. Fried points out that the great danger is this—*when we become numb to pain, we become numb to pleasure as well.* "We pay dearly for the self-induced numbness, for while it relieves our pain, it also reduces our ability to experience pleasant emotions and respond to pleasant stimulation. Unresponsiveness, like an indiscriminate scythe, mows down the flowers with the weeds."

The man who has become numb to the constant pain of humiliation, has also separated himself from pleasure. He no longer experiences the hurt, but neither does he see the beauty of a summer day, delight in the playfulness of his children, or respond to the sexual love that his wife offers. His sexual life will undoubtedly suffer. He will, most likely, become impotent.

And how does woman help him relieve the numbness and return to sensuality? By following the same steps for breaking down his reserve. But in this case it takes a much longer time.

IN THE WORKING WORLD

Woman isn't the only contributor to man's humiliation. In the working world his pride is often brutally cut down. His ability may be questioned. In some companies backbiting is common. Some sadistic employers may undermine an employee. Then there is the struggle for position in which men sometimes discredit one another. Often it is a creditor, or a customer who offers cutting remarks. Some workers are derided by their superiors.

But it is the sum total of his hurt that is injurious. If he comes home to a wife who will heal his wounds he can usually withstand permanent damage; but if he comes home to further humiliation, his entire personality suffers.

MISTAKES WOMEN MAKE

Often women's belittling takes the form of humor. But men are usually too proud to let them know how much it hurts. Women therefore keep up their jibes in innocence.

In moments of anger, women wield their deepest blow—and often they are too emotionally upset to hold any restraint.

But *it is by indifference that woman wounds man most frequently*. By only a yawn, or an expression of the face, or a glance out the window does she show this indifferent attitude. Her refusal to give him full attention—to set aside her household chores when he is exposing some masculine thought—will cut his pride.

Other mistakes are veiled in mystery. How often does she

make some innocent statement, only to have him wince, as if struck by a lash. And doesn't she respond by saying, "Now what did I say that was wrong?"

It is important that you *understand man* fully if you are to avoid crushing his pride. To help you, I have given the following experiences:

EXAMPLE OF RIDICULE

A man told his wife of his idea for an invention to turn the pages of piano music. She said (laughingly), "Oh, no, did you know that Major Hoople recently invented one just like that?" She told the incident to friends and each time succeeded in getting a laugh.

Her husband also thought of a revolutionary design for the common branding iron but due to his wife's ridicule, he failed to carry it out. Several years later the same idea was developed by someone else and proved successful. Even this failed to stop her and she has carried on her humorous ridicule through the years. It isn't difficult to imagine the crushing effect it had on her husband's pride.

RIDICULE

A man presented an idea to his wife for a business investment. She said, "Well, if you want to lose all your money, go ahead."

Another woman used the "cold water" method. Her husband had a novel idea for sports equipment. She was more cautious and said, "Let's be sensible about this."

BELITTLED

Many years ago I knew a girl who was engaged to marry a man of outstanding ability. He appeared to love her dearly but broke the engagement and married someone else. For years it seemed a mystery to those who knew the couple, but later I learned the truth. She lost him because she belittled him. She laughed at his big ideas, made fun of his actions on the basketball court, and joked about his performance in plays. Such a constant eroding of his pride was more than he could stand. This man has become extremely successful, which indicates that in his young years he must have had a tremendous ego.

BELITTLED

A woman gave me the following account: "My husband taught a Sunday School class, and he did it very well. One day I suggested that he ask our son to give part of the lesson in the form of visual aids.

"My husband turned to me and said, with aggravated tone, 'What's the matter, don't you like the way I do it?' I answered, 'Well, you could do better!' "

He became extremely violent, told me that I had never appreciated him, but constantly belittled his efforts. He rushed out of the house, slammed the door, and didn't come back for several hours."

INDIFFERENCE

I watched a woman stirring gravy on the stove. When her husband arrived home, he came into the kitchen and told her of an incident which happened while he was at work. His boss had commended him on his achievements—which he told her with enthusiasm. She said, "Well, isn't that wonderful! Jimmy, go out and turn off the water." Once again he tried to win her interest, but she said, "Go tell the girls to wash for dinner." The man was completely deflated.

INDIFFERENCE

A man who was a well known singer won acclaim from everyone except his wife. He said to a friend, "I would rather have her proud of me than anyone in the audience—but she never makes a comment."

VEILED IN MYSTERY (BELITTLED)

Often it is difficult for woman to detect her mistake. For illustration: A man was very despondent, so his wife tried to cheer him with loving kindness. Then he unfolded his problem, which was a possible failure in his business. She said, "Don't worry, honey, if you fail in your business it won't matter. I will be content if you merely run a small grocery store."

You would think such a self-sacrificing attitude would be met with appreciation, but it was not. To her surprise he snapped back harshly, "Sometimes you say just the wrong things." Why was his response unappreciative and harsh?

She pictured him as a failure. This was no consolation to him. He couldn't bear to have her think of him in this light. Even the word "merely" was a mistake.

What should she have said? She should have restored his faith in himself. She should have talked success, not failure. Her unwavering belief in his ability to pull out of his problem was what he needed.

A woman must think of her man as a success—even though he isn't one at the moment. Anything less is a blow to his ego.

VEILED IN MYSTERY (INDIFFERENCE)

Often when we try the hardest we make the most serious mistakes. A drama teacher of a college began the production of a play. He seldom asked his wife to help, but on this occasion he did ask her to help with the costumes. She worked long hours on them—and they were beautiful. But she noticed a growing antagonism on his part. One evening he said to her, "You are not interested in me." She was both surprised and hurt. She couldn't understand such lack of appreciation.

Her failure was in her consuming interest in the costumes rather than her husband. Here was her man, her hero in action—hoping that she would notice his talent as a director, organizer, and a teacher. He wanted her to notice him as a terrifically successful man.

She, however, felt that he really needed her assistance—that the success of the play partly rested on her shoulders. She didn't realize that the secret reason he had asked her to help was to win her admiration. Certainly he expected her to help with the costumes, but he wanted her to admire him at the same time.

Remember that *the cry of a man's soul is for admiration.* When you show indifference towards this precious need—his love for you will lessen.

You cannot earn his celestial love if you show *contempt, ridicule, or indifference* towards his masculine ability.

And you cannot become Angela Human if you wound his soul.

REWARDS

When you break down a man's reserve you will have every opportunity to understand him and admire him. There will be

a closeness that cannot otherwise exist. You will find yourself
one step nearer to his celestial love.

ASSIGNMENT

If your husband is reserved, take the necessary step to break
down his wall. When you notice that he is particularly withdrawn, be tender and assure him of your love and admiration
for him. Pat his cheek and be soft and affectionate.

CHAPTER VI

Sympathetic Understanding

We have already gained a partial understanding of man, for we know of his great need to be accepted at face value, his longing for appreciation of his manhood, and his very sensitive pride. However, if we are to have true sympathetic understanding, we must know even more about him.

1. HIS PRESSING RESPONSIBILITIES

We must know more about his life, and the pressure and strain he faces from day to day. An excellent description of this is found in Dr. Marie N. Robinson's book, *The Power of Sexual Surrender.*

"For the majority of men, when they come of age and marry, take on an enormous burden which they may not lay down with any conscience this side of the grave. Quietly, and without histrionics, they put aside, in the name of love, most of their vaunted freedom, and contract to take upon their shoulders full social and economic responsibility for their wives and children.

"As a woman, consider for a moment how you would feel if your child should be deprived of the good things of life; proper housing, clothing, education. Consider how you would feel if he should go hungry. Perhaps such ideas have occurred to you and have given you a bad turn momentarily. But they are passing thoughts; a woman does not give them much credence; they are not her direct responsibility; certainly she does not worry about them for long.

"But such thoughts, conscious or unconscious, are her husband's daily fare. He knows and he takes the carking thought to work with him each morning (and every morning) and to bed with him at night, that upon the success or failure of his efforts rest the happiness, health, indeed the very lives of his wife and children. In the ultimate he senses he alone must take full responsibility for them.

"I do not think it is possible to exaggerate how seriously men take this responsibility; how much they worry about it. Women, unless they are very close to their men, rarely know how heavily the burden weighs sometimes, for men talk about it very little. They do not want their loved ones to worry.

"Men have been shouldering the entire responsibility for their family group since earliest times. I often think, however, when I see the stresses and strains of today's market place, that civilized man has much harder going, psychologically speaking, than his primitive forefathers.

"In the first place, the competition creates a terrible strain on the individual male. This competition is not only for preferment and advancement, it is often for his very job itself. Every man knows that if he falters, lets up his ceaseless drive, he can and will be easily replaced.

"No level of employment is really free of this endless pressure. The executive must meet and exceed his last year's quota or the quota of his competitors. Those under him must see that he does it, and he scrutinizes their performance most severely, and therefore constantly.

"Professional men—doctors, lawyers, professors—are under no less pressure for the most part. If the lawyer is self-employed he must constantly seek new clients; if he works for an organization he must exert himself endlessly to avoid being superseded by ambitious peers or by pushing young particles just out of law school and filled with the raw energy of youth. A score of unhappy contingencies can ruin or seriously threaten a doctor's practice, not the least of which is a possible breakdown in his ability to practice. A teacher must work long hours on publishable projects outside of his arduous teaching assignments if he is to advance or even hold his ground.

"There is no field of endeavor that a man may enter where he can count on complete economic safety; competition, the need for unremitting year-in year-out performance is his life's lot. Over all this he knows, too, stands a separate spectre upon which he can exert only the remotest control. It is the joblessness which may be caused by the cyclical depressions and recessions that characterize our economy."

2. His Desire for Status

There is a parallel to his struggle to provide, and it is called struggle for status. This driving desire is noticeable in all male members of the animal kingdom. Robert Ardrey, in his book, *African Genesis,* states that in the animal world the instinct for status, for the acquisition and defense of territory are more compelling for the male than is the sex instinct. The pecking order in the barnyard, the formation in which a flock of wild geese will fly, the hierarchy in a colony of baboons, and the ranking within a herd of elephants is more of a driving force for the male than is the sex function.

This drive for status, or recognition, is evident in the human male. Why do men strive with such fervor to excel, or achieve, or even win a game? Why do they work so diligently for advancement or higher rank? Is the sole purpose money or enjoyment? No! Man has a longing to shine out brightly—to take his place in the world of men.

This drive for superiority over other men is a masculine trait. Women may desire acclaim, but they seldom have tendencies to gain superiority over one another.

Your Hero

Beneath his desire for worldly acclaim lies an even more intense yearning, and it is *his desire to be a hero in your eyes.* It is for this that he lives and breathes.

And yet how many heroes have been honored everywhere except at home. Mrs. Tolstoi didn't recognize her hero. But you can be sure that Mrs. Woodrow Wilson did hers.

When a man is advanced in his job, or earns a higher rank, or learns to fly an airplane, or is applauded for a speech, or a performance on stage, or wins a game—imagine if you can how he would feel if his wife fails to recognize his heroism.

Or imagine how painful for her to esteem some other man a hero—such as a brother, son, father, outstanding man in the community, or even in history. If you want to convince him that he is the hero in your life, *don't use other men as shining examples.*

Why Men Let Down at Home

The drive to provide and the drive for status help to explain why men often let down at home—why they become cross, impatient, and negligent of their duties, their wives, and their children.

Some women say of their husbands, "He doesn't treat his family as well as he does total strangers." When he comes home he is tired of being his best—so he becomes his worst. In Florida Scott-Maxwell's *Women and Sometimes Men,* she explains this tendency of man to show his inferior side:

"One of the poignant paradoxes in the life of a woman is that when a man comes to her, he so often comes to recover his simple humanity, and to rest from being at his best. So a woman frequently has to forego his better side, taking it on trust as a matter of hearsay, and she accepts his lesser side as her usual experience of him. . . . While she wishes to admire him she may lack the knowledge, and perhaps the intelligence to understand the side by which he wins acclaim. She sees him collapse into his home, accepts his need of collapse, indeed receives him with every antenna alert, yet she may forego his superiority with regret. She longs to see his greatness, but has to meet the claim of his smallness."

How Women Show Their Lack
of Sympathetic Understanding

1. *Neglected.* The most frequent complaint I have from women is that they feel neglected.

One girl said that her husband spent most of his time away from home. She had several children, whom she felt she was caring for alone, and she seldom saw her husband.

But upon inquiring, I found that most of his time spent away from home was in working. Also, they were planning to have a large family, and wanted expensive educations and other high goals for their children. He therefore felt it was essential for him to earn a large income by working long hours. It was obvious that she had a lack of sympathy for his motives.

Another woman complained that her husband held down two jobs. He was away most of the time. One day she said: "You are no more than a pay check to me." He was very cut. She didn't realize that he was trying to solve some difficult financial problems.

There are women who complain of their husband's church

activities which take them away for hours at a time. They do not realize that their men are only trying to do their duties. It would help if they would say: *I would rather have ten percent of a hundred percent man, than one hundred percent of a ten percent man.*

2. *Neglect of Home Duties:* Another complaint is the man who will not mow the lawn and do repair jobs, painting, and other duties while home. He is not always justified because of outside pressures. But often women's impatient attitude shows her lack of understanding. This irksome problem, however, will be discussed more fully in chapter 8.

3. *How He Is Greeted When He Arrives Home.* Then there is the woman who greets her husband at the door with problems. And she allows the children to rush at him and offer their share of complaints.

4. *Investments.* Women who don't understand man's struggle for sustenance and status often fight against their husband's desire to invest, or expand their business, or perhaps change occupations. Often the comment is, "Oh, we have everything we need now. We have a home almost paid for, a nice car, and a nice income to live on. And we even have this money saved ahead." Then she might add, "Why are you dissatisfied?" or "Why do you want more?"

She may not realize that he can see further into the future than she can, and can visualize more children, college educations, more expensive clothes as the children mature, and even his decline in productivity as the provider. He wants to make it now and have the money to meet these emergencies.

Or there is the man who already has wealth. His wife might wonder why he is never satisfied. If she gave him the recognition he needed as her hero he might not strive for greater heights.

THE PROPER ATTITUDE

We must realize that man has *mountains to climb,* and *rivers to cross,* and wants to *take his place in the world of men.* He seldom really neglects you or his children. He is only trying to conquer the world and bring it back to you.

And if he spends unnecessary time away from home you have probably driven him to it by your unsympathetic attitude at other times.

When a Man Comes Home from a Day's Work

It is most important that you know how to treat a man when he arrives home. It would be good practice if you train your children to kiss their father upon his arrival, and then lead him by the hand into the bedroom. Have him lie down, take off his shoes and *make him comfortable*. Play relaxing music, and speak with a soothing tone in your voice. Allow him this peace for an ample time before you expose him to the rest of the family. He works to protect and shelter you from harm and want. This is woman's way of bringing comfort to her man.

Forgiveness

Still another way to demonstrate your sympathetic attitude is to overlook many of his thoughtless blunders. Men are often negligent in informing their wives that they will be late for dinner. They also forget birthdays, and anniversaries. They will keep a woman waiting, fail to remember a dinner engagement, or an important errand that she requested. Your sympathy will make forgiveness easy and will remove a millstone from his neck.

Rewards

Don't think that he will take unfair advantage of your sympathetic attitude. This sort of kindness brings back double in return. And it plays its part in awakening a holy feeling of Celestial love in his heart, as in the following experience:

Success Story

"My marriage has really been wonderful since applying the principles of this philosophy. The other day when my husband came home from work tired, I applied sympathetic understanding. I made him comfortable and treated him like a king. He smiled directly at me and said, 'Sweetheart, for the first time in almost seven years, I get butterflies in my stomach when I think about coming home to you.' "

Assignment

Tell him:

"I am beginning to understand the heavy responsibility you have to provide for me and the children. I want you to know that I appreciate it, and that I am sorry I have not done so enough in the past.

"I want to support you in any plans which you might have for our future. I think I understand now some of the goals which you have tried to explain in the past."

SYMPATHY FOR THE DISCOURAGED MAN

I have told you of the sympathy you must have for man's life in general. But now I want to tell you of his special need of sympathy when he is discouraged.

The tendency to be moody, depressed, discouraged is very common among men. Whether great or small, success or failure, learned or ignorant, or any of the degrees in between, few men escape this unpleasant experience. In fact, the more learned, talented, and aggressive men tend to have the most intense suffering.

Many years ago, a young midwestern lawyer suffered such great depression that his friends thought it wise to keep knives and razors out of his reach. This young man wrote, "I am now the most miserable man living. Shall I ever be better? I cannot tell; I awfully forbode I shall not." His name was Abraham Lincoln.

A woman has the power to break man's spell of gloom and restore his soul. Man knows this, and therefore, he turns to woman in this hour of need.

But few women know how to give true sympathy. It isn't that they don't try, but that they don't know how. They make all kinds of mistakes, say just the wrong things and often none of the right. Their greatest mistake is that they try to help him solve his problems—to rescue him—to offer suggestions, or to help lift his burdens, or to remove his obstacles. All of these are mistaken approaches. All of these things hurt his pride.

It isn't practical help he needs from you. He comes to have his soul restored, his self-esteem re-established, and his self-doubt removed.

HOW TO GIVE SYMPATHY

Come to him with warmth and tenderness. Your very approach should be enough to melt his icy mood. If he talks and tells you of his troubles, let him. If not, do not force the issue, for he may be hiding his failures from you. Don't attempt to solve his problems, lift his burdens, or remove his obstacles directly and don't give him advice unless he appears to want it. Then give it only in a feminine way—as I will explain in the next chapter.

Build him up by offering him approval, hope and admiration, and whatever you do, don't let his gloom rub off on you.

Be enthusiastic, hopeful and self-assured, and say, "This is a dark hour that will pass. My belief in your success in the future is unshaken." If he is discouraged for awhile, accept it, and let him know he may have as much time as he needs to overcome his discouragement. Be happy and optimistic regardless, but do not necessarily expect an immediate response in him for your efforts.

One of the functions of woman is to be a comfort to her husband—*To shed joy around, and cast light upon dark days.* Do not fail him in his hour of need.

The quality of true sympathy is rare in women. Because of this, man often learns to do without it—learns to withstand alone the buffets of time and circumstance. But naturally his love for the woman is adversely affected.

It is interesting to note that when a woman is discouraged, she looks to her man—hoping he will help her solve her problems, lift her burdens and remove her obstacles. This is natural, for he is her leader, protector and provider. But men don't want this kind of sympathy from their wives. This difference in temperament between men and women is the very reason why it is so difficult for a woman to understand what kind of sympathy a man wants.

WHEN A MAN HAS FAILED

When a man has failed in his business or in any part of his role as man it becomes a painful crisis in his life. It is not only the failure itself he suffers, but the fear of humiliation in the eyes of his wife.

If his failure is financial and if this loss requires that he lower his standard of living he has an even greater fear. *His protective feeling towards his wife causes him to fear the inconvenience and discomfort his wife may be put to.*

Understanding what he suffers at these moments is a vital

part of our ability to understand men. And knowing just how to respond is a necessary art in becoming Angela Human. An illustration of man's agony on such an occasion and woman's beautiful response is found in Washington Irving's essay, "The Wife."

THE WIFE

"My intimate friend Leslie had married a beautiful and accomplished girl, who had been brought up in the midst of fashionable life. She had, it is true, no fortune; but that of my friend was ample, and he delighted in the anticipation of indulging her in every elegant pursuit and administering to those delicate tastes and fancies that spread a kind of witchery about the sex. 'Her life,' said he, 'shall be like a fairy tale.'

"The very difference in their characters produced a harmonious combination—he was of a romantic and somewhat serious cast; she was all life and gladness. I have often noticed the mute rapture with which he would gaze upon her in company, of which her sprightly powers made her his delight; and how, in the midst of applause, her eye would still turn to him as if there alone she sought favor and acceptance.

"When leaning on his arm, her slender form contrasted finely with his tall, manly person. The fond, confiding air with which she looked up to him seemed to call forth a flush of triumphant pride and cherishing tenderness as if he doted on his lovely burden for its very helplessness. Never did a couple set forward on the flowery path of early and well-suited marriage with a fairer prospect of felicity.

"It was the misfortune of my friend, however, to have embarked his property in large speculations; and he had not been married many months, when, by a succession of sudden disasters, it was swept from him, and he found himself reduced almost to penury. For a time he kept his situation to himself and went about with a haggard countenance and a breaking heart. His life was but a protracted agony; and what rendered it more unsupportable was the necessity of keeping up a smile in the presence of his wife; for he could not bring himself to overwhelm her with the news.

"She saw, however, with the quick eyes of affection, that all was not well with him. She marked his altered looks and stifled sighs and was not to be deceived by his sickly and vapid attempts at cheerfulness. She tasked all her sprightly powers and tender blandishments to win him back to happiness; but she only drove the arrow deeper into his soul. The more he saw cause to love her, the more torturing was the thought that he was soon to make her wretched.

"A little while, thought he, and the smile will vanish from that cheek—the song will die away from those lips—the luster of those eyes will be quenched with sorrow; and the happy heart which now beats lightly in that bosom will be weighed down like mine, with the cares and miseries of the world. At length he came to me, one day, and related his whole situation, in a tone of the deepest despair.

"When I had heard him through I inquired, 'Does your wife know all this?' At the question he burst into an agony of tears. 'For God's sake!' cried he, 'if you have any pity on me, don't mention my wife; it is the thought of her that drives me almost to madness!' 'And why not?' said I. 'She must know it sooner or later; you can not keep it long from her, and the intelligence may break upon her in a more startling manner than if imparted by yourself; for the accents of those we love soften the harshest tidings.

" 'Besides, you are depriving yourself of the comforts of her sympathy; and not merely that, but also endangering the only bond that can keep hearts together—unreserved community of thought and feeling. She will soon perceive that something is secretly preying upon your mind; and true love will not brook reserve; it feels undervalued and outraged when even the sorrows of those it loves are concealed from it.'

" 'Oh, but my friend! to think what a blow I am to give to all her future prospects—how I am to strike her very soul to the earth, by telling her that her husband is a beggar! that she is to forego all the elegances of life—all the pleasures of society—to shrink with me into indigence and obscurity! To tell her that I have dragged her down from the sphere in which she might have continued to move in constant brightness, the light of every eye, the admiration of every heart! How can she bear poverty? She has been brought up in all the refinements of opulence. How can she bear neglect? She had been the idol of society. Oh! it will break her heart—it will break her heart!'

"After additional patience, the friend finally persuaded Leslie to go home and unburden his sad heart to his wife. The next morning the friend was eager to know the results. In inquiring, he found that Leslie had made the disclosure.

" 'And how did she bear it?' 'Like an angel! It seemed rather to be a relief to her mind, for she threw her arms round my neck, and asked if this was all that had lately made me unhappy. But, poor girl!' added he, 'she can not realize the change we must undergo. She has no idea of poverty but in the abstract; she has only read of it in poetry, where it is allied to love.

" 'She feels yet no privation; she suffers no loss of accustomed conveniences. When we come practically to experience its sordid cares, its paltry wants, its petty humiliations, then will be the real trial.'

"Some days afterward he called upon me in the evening. He had disposed of his dwelling house, and taken a small cottage in the country, a few miles from town. He had been busied all day in sending out furniture. The new establishment required few articles, and those of the simplest kind.

"He was going out to the cottage where his wife had been all day superintending its arrangement. My feelings had become strongly interested in the progress of the family story, and as it was evening, I offered to accompany him. He was wearied with the fatigues of the day, and as he walked out, fell into a fit of gloomy musing.

" 'Poor Mary!' at length broke, with a heavy sigh from his lips. 'And what of her?' asked I; 'has anything happened to her?' 'What!' said he, darting an impatient glance; 'is it nothing to be reduced to this paltry situation—to be caged in a miserable cottage—to be obliged to toil almost in the menial concerns of her wretched habitation?'

" 'Has she, then, repined at the change?' 'Repined! she has been nothing but sweetness and good-humor. Indeed, she seems in better spirits than I have ever known her; she has been to me all love and tenderness and comfort!' 'Admirable girl!' exclaimed I. 'You call yourself poor, my friend; you never were so rich—you never knew the boundless treasures of excellence you possess in that woman.'

" 'Oh! but, my friend, if this, our first meeting at the cottage were over, I think I could then be comfortable. But this is her first day of real experience; she has been introduced into a humble dwelling; she has been employed all day in arranging its miserable equipments; she has for the first time, known fatigues of domestic employment; she has, for the first time looked around her on a home destitute of everything elegant—almost everything convenient; and now may be sitting down exhausted and spiritless, brooding over a prospect of future poverty.'

There was a degree of probability in this picture that I could not gainsay; so we walked on in silence. After turning from the main road up a narrow lane, so thickly shaded with forest-trees as to give it a complete air of seclusion, we came in sight of the cottage. It was humble enough in its appearance for the most pastoral poet; and yet it had a pleasing rural look. A wild vine had overrun one end with a profusion of foliage; a few trees threw their branches gracefully over it; and I observed several pots of flowers tastefully disposed about the door, and on the grass-plot in front.

"A small wicket gate opened upon a foot-path that wound through some shrubbery to the door. Just as we approached, we heard the sound of music. Leslie grabbed my arm, we paused and listened. It was Mary's voice, singing in a style of the most touching simplicity, a little air of which her husband was peculiarly fond. I felt Leslie's hand tremble on my arm. He stepped forward, to hear more distinctly. His step made a noise on the gravel-walk.

"A bright, beautiful face glanced out of the window and vanished, a light footstep was heard, and Mary came tripping forth to meet us. She was in a pretty rural dress of white; a few wild-flowers were twisted in her fine hair; a fresh bloom was on her cheek; her whole countenance beamed with smiles—I had never seen her look so lovely.

" 'My dear Leslie,' cried she, 'I am so glad you are come! I have been watching and watching for you; and running down the lane, and looking for you. I've set out a table under a beautiful tree behind the cottage; and I've been gathering some of the most delicious strawberries, for I know you are fond of them—and we have such excellent cream—and everything is so sweet and still here! Oh!' said she, putting her arm within his, and looking up brightly in his face—'oh, we shall be so happy.'

"Poor Leslie was overcome. He caught her to his bosom, he folded his arms around her, he kissed her again and again; he could not speak, but the tears gushed into his eyes; and he has often assured me that, though the world has since gone prosperously with him, and his life has, indeed, been a happy one, yet never has he experienced a moment of more exquisite felicity."

This account of Washington Irving's is an illustration of what intense suffering a man can experience when he faces financial disaster. Mary's response is heavenly, and an illustration of our ideal of Angela Human.

It may be a residence less attractive than a cottage in the woods a woman must face. Suppose it is an extremely unattractive house in a crowded city or in a dry desolate desert country. But these extremes only deepen man's appreciation when his wife accepts her humble circumstances with Mary's attitude—thus bringing him comfort and true sympathy.

ASSIGNMENT

1. Say, "I am beginning to understand the heavy responsibility you have to provide for me and the children. I want you to know that I appreciate it, and that I am sorry I have not done so enough in the past."

2. If he is discouraged or depressed, approach him as I have suggested, with a spirit of optimist and cheerfulness, suggesting something like this: "This is a dark hour that will pass. I feel certain that you will be able to overcome your problem and discouragement."

CHAPTER VII

Man's Role in Life

MAN'S DESIRE TO BE SUPERIOR IN HIS ROLE AS MAN

What is the role of man? It is to be the *guide, protector, and provider* for his wife and children. This is his natural role and belongs to him by right.

1. *Guide.* There is ample proof that man is the intended leader of his family. The first commandment which God gave unto woman was, *"thy desire shall be unto thy husband, and he shall rule over thee."* The Apostle Paul tells us that woman is to *"reverence"* her husband and he says, *"Submit yourselves unto your own husbands."* The Apostle Peter tells us *"Ye wives, be in subjection to your own husbands."* The Apostle Paul compared man's leadership of his wife to Christ's leadership of the church. *"For the husband is the head of the wife, even as Christ is the head of the church. Therefore, as the church is subject unto Christ, so let the wives be to their own husbands in everything."*

A latter day prophet has also emphasized the father's time honored position. "There is no higher authority in matters relating to the family organization than that of the father. The Patriarchal Order is of divine origin and will continue through time and eternity. In the home the presiding authority is always vested in the father, and in all home affairs and family matters there is no other authority paramount."

2. *Protector.* When we compare man's body build and his superior muscular strength with the fragile structure of woman, we cannot deny that man was also created to be her protector.

3. *Provider.* The first commandment which God gave unto man was, "In the sweat of thy face shalt thou eat bread, till thou return unto the ground." He gave this commandment not to Eve, but to Adam.

(Genesis 3:16, Eph. 5:33, Col. 3:18, I Pet. 3:1, Genesis 3:19, Eph. 5:23-24.)

MAN'S NATIVE ABILITY

Not only was man assigned the responsibility of leading, protecting and providing for his family—but he was given the native ability to fulfill this duty. He was made for the stresses and strains of the market place, has the facility to make weighty decisions, and was blessed with both strength and endurance to protect his family from all harm. Woman was created for a different kind of strain and endurance—far different from man's.

THE PARTNERSHIP

We have often heard the statement, "marriage is a partnership." But what kind of a partnership? It is not an equal partnership, for man's role is to be guide, protector, and provider, whereas woman's is loving wife, mother, and homemaker. Man and woman are not partners in leadership, nor motherhood, nor homemaking. With thought we can see that although man's and woman's role are equal in importance they are not equal in responsibility.

In *Marriage for Moderns,* by Henry A. Bowman, this unequal partnership is compared to a lock and key. Man and woman, he tells us, are like a lock and a key which join together to form a functioning unit. "Together they can accomplish something that neither acting alone can accomplish. Nor can it be accomplished by two locks or two keys. Each is distinct; yet neither is complete in and of itself. Their roles are neither identical nor interchangeable. Neither is superior to the other, since both are necessary. They are equally important. Each must be judged in terms of its own function. They are complementary." Marriage then is a complementary partnership.

MAN'S BURNING DESIRE

What must we learn of man's role if we are to become as Agnes? We must understand *his desire to be superior in his role as man.* It is only in his role as man that he longs for supremacy over woman. He does not desire to excel her in her domestic role, or her role as mother. Nothing gives him a more enjoyable sense of power and manliness than does this supremacy. Therefore, if he does not feel superior now, woman must make him feel so.

I have outlined the steps to understanding man and have said that they are:

1. Acceptance
2. Admiration
3. Pride
4. Sympathetic understanding
5. Desire for superiority in his masculine role.

Man, the Guide

Every organization is designed with a leader at its head, whether it be captain, governor, or president. This is a matter of law and order. Therefore, the family, a group of intelligent beings, must be organized else chaos will result. It does not matter how large or small the family, even though it be just man and wife, there still needs to be a leader.

A woman who steals her husband's leadership robs him of his rightful experience in this life. If he is incapable then he must become capable.

Duties of the Leader or Guide

1. *To dictate the policies, rules and laws for the family to follow.* He may choose to delegate some of his authority to his wife, or he may call the entire family together for discussion to get their ideas, but ultimately the right to dictate is his. His word should be law. This is neither harsh nor unfair. It is entirely a matter of law and order.

The right to establish rules of conduct, use of the family car, expenditure of family funds, where the family spends its vacation, church attentance, which schools the children will attend are ultimately his to say. This may seem unfair, but someone must have the final word in the matter. Should woman dictate?

What should you do when his policies clash with your religious convictions? Should you follow him in what you consider "unrighteousness?" Whether you yourself follow is your own choice, but remember man's children are *his* sheep. He must rule over his flock. Even though your husband be of another religion he has right of supremacy over his children.

The father is the head, or president, or spokesman of the family. This arrangement is of divine origin. It is not merely a question of who is perhaps the best qualified (the man or the wife). Neither is it wholly a question of who is living the most worthy life. It is a question largely of law and order, and its importance is seen often from the fact that the authority remains and is respected long after the man is really unworthy to exercise it.

And if woman is reasonable, she will go along with his ideas, though she may share an opposite viewpoint—*unless his policies are wicked. And if a man becomes wicked—would teach his children to lie, or cheat or steal—she should take them out of his household. But as long as she remains under his roof she should honor his authority to rule.*

When man rules there is a state of peace which cannot otherwise exist. It relieves both wife and children of any thought to "argue a point." A woman can relax, stop trying to wield her influence where it is neither needed or wanted, and can turn attention to her pressing duties.

2. *To make decisions in his masculine duties.* In his role as leader, man will naturally face many decisions, both large and small. Here again, the father may choose to call in his family for council. If so, they may express themselves. But if he decides against their opinion it is his right. If he does not choose to council his family, even his wife, it is his right, and his decision should be respected.

How Decisions are Made in Many Families

a. *By the woman:* It is surprising in how many families women make the major decisions. Why don't men protest against this infringement? They sometimes even encourage it. Often it is due to early experiences of having domineering mothers who ran the household at home. Or they may have been reared by a widow who had the role of leadership forced upon her. In either case, the men have a false picture of how things ought to be, and so the practice of woman's rule continues from one generation to the next and becomes increasingly common.

b. *By mutual agreement:* In some marriages decisions are reached by "mutual agreement." But if man and wife do not agree, they let matters rest until they do—which may be never. This is an inefficient way to run an organization, for no one has the right to a final say or to take action. Woman has the power of the veto which is the power to stop man's action.

When a man allows this, he delegates authority to his wife which is equal to his own. Such is the power of our U.S. President, and his right to veto decisions, or laws, and send them back to Congress for reconsideration. This way of reaching decisions may be all right for Congress, but it is an inefficient way for a man to run his household. It bogs him down. He always has to go through "official channels." He can't run his life with full authority and freedom.

The wife is put to equal disadvantage. Whether she makes the decisions, or shares equally in making them, she is weighted down with responsibility, thoughts and worries which should not be hers, and which she was not designed to carry, and which make her life difficult.

When Woman Rules

When woman rules, it robs her of presence of mind to do her homemaking tasks well. Generally speaking it is trying on a woman's emotions to assume the leadership role. But if she develops capabilities which make these masculine duties easy for her—*she tends to lose some of her essential feminine charm.*

When Man Rules

When a man assumes his full role as leader he is more free to make decisions and plans efficiently. He knows he can move ahead without obstacles. He knows that when a particular decision of his does not make sense, he will not have to explain it to his wife. Or he knows that when he consults her he can disregard her opinion if he chooses, and she will not resent him for it He knows that although his wife trusts him she does not expect perfection and will allow for his mistakes.

When man is leader, life is easier, more orderly, and there is a more fertile field for love to grow.

It may seem easy for you to agree that the role of leadership belongs to man, and you may even be anxious to have him assume it completely. You may, in fact, want very much to be relieved of the burden of making weighty decisions. Is it that easy? Do you just toss him the ball and then wait for everything to fall into place?

Man Turns to Woman

If man ruled with wisdom, strength and determination, he could dictate and you could follow. But his load grows heavy, and his decisions are difficult and hence, he turns to woman for her feminine insight.

The question is, "should his wife refuse to help him and encourage him to make his decisions and plans independent of her? Or if she does help, how can she do so without stepping back into the pants of the family?"

Woman's Part in Leadership

Woman does have a part to play in leadership but a very feminine part. It need not be an undue strain on her nor detract from the man's ego.

1. *Feminine Insight.* Women are fountains of wisdom and have insight or intuition that is unique with their sex. Also, they have a different perspective—a feminine perspective—of their husband's activities that no other person has. Therefore, their "woman's intuition" may prove valuable when desperately needed.

Mumtaz, queen of the Taj Mahal, played a part in her husband's leadership. She was well educated, and the daughter of the Primes Minister. "Her husband consulted her in many of his technical matters of government."

2. *Feminine Impulse.* Should you give forth your intuition when not asked? If you feel an impulse to do so, then it is advisable.

You will remember that during the trials of Jesus, Pilate's wife sent a message to him when he was sitting in the judgement seat, saying, "Have thou nothing to do with that just man: for I have suffered many things this day in a dream because of him."

Your opinion might save a crisis, but express it in the following manner:

How to Give Feminine Advice

Give forth advice as a "fountain" that bubbles over in a park. One can take as much or as little as he pleases, or may choose to stand back and admire the beauty of the fountain itself. Use the "take it or leave it" approach and let him drink as much or as little as he likes. Use the words "I feel," or "I believe," for they are indicative of insight.

Make no effort to insist upon your point of view or to convince him, or explain why you feel as you do. And remember the following don'ts:

1. *Don't appear to know more than he does.* Don't map out a course for him to follow, analyze his problem or decision, or make a lot of suggestions.

2. *Don't be motherly.* Don't take the attitude, "Here is this poor little boy in the world who isn't getting along so well, and I must come to his rescue and help him."

3. *Don't talk man to man.* Don't hash things over as men do, and thereby place yourself on an equal plane with him. Don't say, "I think I have spotted the trouble area," or "Why don't we go over this, or that," or "Let's come to some conclusions."

In giving feminine advice remember: *Make him feel superior in his role as leader.*

Once you have given him advice you must be willing to take what comes and recognize his authority to disregard your advice if he chooses.

Such a feminine contribution on woman's part is not burdensome to her. In the first place, she does not go into all the pros and cons and pitfalls of the matter, and in the second place, she knows that the weight of the decision or plan rests upon her husband.

WOMAN'S SUPPORTING ROLE

When man is dominant and woman agrees with his leadership ideas, harmony in marriage is easy. But, this is not always the case. The following are problems which arise:

1. *When woman doesn't agree.* How can you support an idea with which you do not agree. Remember this: You are not supporting the idea—but the man making it. You do this just as you support a president, or chairman, or superintendent who takes some action against your judgment.

You might say to your husband, *"I do not agree with your plan, but I want you to follow your own convictions, and I will support you in it, whatever the outcome."* Then if he chooses his own opinion, compliment his manliness by saying, "I am glad that you had the courage of your convictions and did what you thought best."

Women often disagree with their men. Why? Because they are afraid. They fear that their husbands might lose their money, or fail in business, or get into difficulty. Or it may be regret, disappointment, or unhappiness that they fear. And yet, what man ever climbed to the top of the mountain without running this risk? What man ever succeeded without his share of failures? Let us examine Abraham Lincoln's record for success.

When he was a young man he ran for the legislature in Illinois and was defeated. He next entered business and failed and spent seventeen years of his life paying up the debts of a worthless partner. Entering politics, he ran for Congress and was defeated. Then he tried an appointment in the U.S. Land Office but failed. He became candidate for the U.S. Senate and was again defeated. In 1856, he became a candidate for the Vice Presidency and was again defeated. In 1858 he lost the election to Douglas. Yet he eventually achieved the highest success attainable in public life. The life of a successful man is often so mixed with failure that it causes us to feel failure to be a necessary obstacle on the road to success.

The way to overcome your fears is to obtain an attitude of "willingness to take risks." Be willing to take chances, and give him the freedom to make mistakes if necessary. Don't spend a lot of time thinking about the outcome of his decisions, but rather board up your mind against them, and *have a girlish trust in him.* A happy marriage is worth more than material success.

2. *When a man flounders.* How can you support a man when he cannot make up his mind? Some men fluctuate back and forth because it is their nature to do so. They are cautious and choose this route to making decisions. If so, they should be allowed their freedom to be themselves and should be "accepted at face value."

But at times it is a particular fear that stands in his way, one that a woman needs to understand. He may fear that his decision may threaten the security or the comfort of his family, as in the case of a man returning to school for further education, or cutting expenses to expand his business. In this case, his wife should encourage the decision by reassuring him that she is willing to make the noble sacrifice.

At other times he flounders because he fears loss of money, loss of prestige or failure. He may desire to proceed with his plan, but lacks the courage to do so. If his fears are groundless, you should re-establish his confidence by *building up his ego.* Offer him the reassurance that he does have the abilities and qualifications which he may feel at the time are lacking. But in helping him overcome his fears, *don't act braver than he.*

I know of a case in which the woman made this mistake. The man was about to make a change in both business and residence but the last minute he started dragging his feet. He wanted to proceed, but fears of every description stood in his way. In her efforts to encourage him, his wife said, "Why are you hesitating? You have nothing to be afraid of?"

She should have said, "Dear, I know just how you must feel. There are so many problems and unknown factors that enter in. You really have reason to hesitate. If it were me, I couldn't make such a big decision. How do you endure the responsibility of being a man?"

Such meekness on her part would probably have awakened his heroism and caused him to say, "It isn't so tough; I think I can handle the situation."

Remember, in giving him advice, or in supporting him: *make him feel superior as the leader.*

How to Help a Man Become a Good Leader

While you are helping your husband and supporting him you can at the same time, be inspiring him to become a strong leader by applying the following rules:

1. *Discuss his leadership role with him.* Convince him that he belongs there by right, is God ordained, and fully qualified.

2. *Be efficient in your own domestic role.* By doing so, you more clearly define the division of responsibilities, and he will hesitate to lean on you unduly.

3. *Be feminine when consulted on major decisions.* It is feminine to flounder and flutter in making weighty decisions. I am told that in the real estate business a man will invariably make a firm decision if his wife is indecisive. It makes man feel superior.

4. *Notice and comment on his superior capabilities as a leader.* Admire his judgement, his decisiveness, his cleverness. Your belief in him is essential to his confidence.

5. *Be a good follower by doing the following:*

    a. Don't have a lot of preconceived ideas which may clash

with your husband's manly dreams or masculine responsibilities—such as where you want to live, plans for children, etc.

b. Make all of your dreams portable. Woman should learn to be happy anywhere, in any circumstance—on a mountain top, or on burning desert, in poverty's vale, or abounding in wealth.

c. *Have a girlish trust in him,* just as a child does towards his parents.

6. *Let go.* Let him have full reign and do not stand back with anxiety wondering if things will turn out all right. If he makes mistakes, gets into difficulty, let him suffer the consequences. It is the only way he will learn.

7. *Let him know you enjoy following, and not leading.* If you do, he will be anxious to keep you happy by continuing to assume the burden of leadership.

But it isn't enough to help him become a leader—you must *make him feel superior in his role as leader.*

WHEN WOMAN STANDS IN HIS WAY

Serious marriage difficulties may arise when a woman "puts her foot down" and refuses to follow her husband's leadership.

Years ago, I knew a woman who refused to move from the community in which she and her husband lived, on the grounds that it might be a disadvantage to their children. The man was extremely disappointed, for he felt the move would be an advantage in his occupation. He did not become successful in the community in which he remained, and felt that had he moved his life would have turned out better.

He felt thwarted. Because of this he developed a resentful attitude towards his wife and started arguments over trivial matters. She thought the move would harm her children, but she did them a greater injustice by putting a wedge in her marriage.

Another reason woman stands in man's way is her fear of his failure. But, *it is better to let him have his way and fail, than to stand in his way and have him feel thwarted.*

Occasionally a man will give credit to his wife for putting her foot down and thus keeping him from making a mistake. He may even thank her for it. Don't let this confuse you. Just let her stand in his way when the outcome would have been a glorious success and see if he thanks her for it. It is a grave risk woman takes when she stands in her husband's way.

I want to remind you again of the rewards which will come to you in your steps to becoming Angela Human. At times it may seem like effort and drastic changes are required. But remember that I am trying to teach you how to become a woman—the kind a man wants and the kind you were designed to be. As a result, you will earn his Celestial love. Isn't this worth your whole hearted determination? The great glories are not earned without labor. The following success stories will demonstrate such rewards:

SUCCESS STORY

"After learning Fascinating Womanhood, I decided to keep out of my husband's rulings over the children. The other day our son wanted to play with the children in the park. His father said, 'No!' He came crying to me but I said it was up to his father whether he could go or not. After awhile, my husband came to me and asked if I thought he should let him go and I answered, 'It's up to you.' He did let him go and the rest of the day was such a happy one. If I hadn't honored his leadership it would have ended up with all of us angry and not speaking."

SUCCESS STORY

"I had fought for everything I wanted in marriage (great and small) and gotten nowhere. One morning we were going out of town with our children and I wanted to go to the corner beauty salon to have my hair combed. My husband said 'No! We have to leave immediately.' (We had no reason to hurry.) I said, 'It will only take ten minutes,' but he still said no. But this time I honored his word and went. On the way I felt resentful and bitter.

"On the way I began to reason with myself, knowing I must honor his leadership, accept him at face value and look to his better side. I said to myself, 'If he doesn't care how I look, why should I? He is the most important person in my life.' Soon I relaxed and became more cheerful and began visiting with him. (It was an effort.) Then this surprising thing happened: As soon as we arrived at our destination, he drove to a beauty salon and kept the family waiting in the car while I had my hair combed. He has never done anything like this before." She said this with tears in her eyes.

(Why do men say "no" so much? Often it is just to show their authority! Men usually want to be fair and generous with their families, but when their leadership has been trampled on, they know of no other way to appear as leader than to stand in opposition. If women would honor their husband's right to rule, men would be more reasonable.)

Family Finances

Both man and wife share in responsibility of family finances. Man, in his duties as leader and provider—woman in hers as wife and homemaker share this function. But many have the parts they play confused. The proper division of concern is this:

FINANCIAL RESPONSIBILITY

Man's	Woman's
1. Provide money	1. Support his financial plans
2. Manage money	2. Provide peaceful home life
3. *Necessary worry*	3. *Make a dollar stretch*

If you were to reduce these duties down to those most essential, they would be:

Man's: TO WORRY—Woman's: TO MAKE A DOLLAR STRETCH

Yet, what do we find? Many men think their only duty is to provide the living. They hand their paycheck over to their wives with the words, "Here, make it do." So she struggles and she saves and manages to accumulate a few savings. Who does the worrying? She does!

And since her husband is the leader, he reaches into the bank account and uses the savings for investments and luxuries. And he does so without consulting her. Doesn't he have this right? Isn't he the leader? If he would assume the full role as leader and give his wife her fair allotment, then he would have the right, *but not otherwise.*

In other homes we find a different situation. Woman works to help provide the living. At times her home is in confusion, and her man cannot think straight. No wonder he cannot manage his money problems, and no wonder he is a poor provider.

And yet in other homes, we find that although the man worries, although he provides and tries to manage his money, he always has financial problems for *he has an extravagant wife.*

What are the solutions to these problems? One is the recognition of their rightful roles. The other is the two separate budgets.

The Separate Budget

The most sensible solution to common money problems between husband and wife is a fair budget for the wife to run her household on. If she has money left over it should be hers to use as she wishes. When she has this incentive—she naturally becomes thrifty.

The man should have all above this to manage with his own discretion. If he has an excess it should be his to say. He may wish to consult his wife regarding savings or investments, but if he does not, as the leader it is his right of decision. If he squanders his money it is also his right, and woman does not have the right to interfere *as long as she has a fair budget* for the needs of her household which includes the children.

Dangers When Woman Manages Entire Budget

A couple I know had their responsibilities confused. Each time he received a pay check he handed it to his wife. She managed it very well until several more children came along. It became increasingly difficult to cover expenses and she began to almost break with worry. She tried to explain some of their problems, but he was not used to thinking about them.

An opportunity arose in which the man was offered a higher paying position if he would move to a different state. When husband and wife considered the decision mutually, the wife wanted to move, for she could see the solutions to their financial problems, but the husband—being the leader—refused. He was happy with conditions as they were. So they remained, but the wife for years had an unfair share of worry.

If the woman is to handle the entire paycheck she need also

have the leader's right to decisions which concern their financial life; otherwise it is not fair. The harm that comes to both husband and wife when woman carries the financial burden is:

1. *Harm to man.* It robs him of his rightful masculine role for which he need feel supremacy. Also, it causes him to make poor decisions, because he is unfamiliar with the problems.

2. *Harm to woman.* The most serious harm comes to the woman.

A woman told me that before she applied this philosophy she was "sick with worry" and was afraid of losing her health. Women do not have the temperament to take such emotional worry. And if they become capable of doing so—they lose some of their womanly charm. If your man does not realize what a burden financial worry is to you, then you should tell him.

WHAT IF I HAND HIM THE BURDEN OF FINANCES AND HE MAKES A MESS OF THINGS

A woman told me that she followed my advice and handed finances to her husband. She was relieved at first, but soon she realized that he was making a total mess of things. He was behind in the house payments, couldn't manage the bills, and was at times overdrawn in their bank account. She said, "I am a nervous wreck! I don't want the job back, but I don't know what to do!"

HOW TO DO IT

When a woman gives a man the financial load she should *let go* and turn her back on it completely. If he makes a mess of things for awhile let him suffer the consequences—no matter what they are. If you do, he will learn by experience. Remember, if you have been handling it he has been robbed of his rightful experience and will have to learn by doing.

And it is important to let him know how happy you are to be rid of the load. If you act anxious and worried about his management, he will probably like it better the way it was before and give the load back to you. But if you act relieved and happy he will want to keep you that way and will make every effort to improve in his new responsibility.

THE KEEPING OF THE BOOKS

It is naturally more ideal if man keeps the books. But as

long as he is aware of his financial problems it is not essential. If he assigns woman to be his accountant it need not be a problem.

When man assumes financial duty, as in other phases of leadership, *it makes him feel superior in his role.* This is vital to him, although he may not now realize it.

Success Story (Finances)

"In the past I have tried to handle the finances in the family, since my husband has been very irresponsible about money. You just can't imagine how foolish he has been—spending his money on motorcycles and other luxuries, always negligent about paying bills, and never able to hang on to any money.

"After studying Fascinating Womanhood, I became convinced that I should hand over the finances to him regardless. It was a risky feeling, but he was willing to do it. To my surprise—even amazement, he has become a changed man; is responsible and thrifty with his money and has developed leadership qualities. He now manages our money better than I used to."

Success Story (Finances)

"For years my husband has wanted a tractor to keep up our $2\frac{1}{2}$ acres of land, but I have always 'raised the roof' and said 'No.' Since taking the Fascinating Womanhood course I decided to relax. After all he is the provider.

"The other day our lawn mower broke and he started talking about a tractor again. I said, 'Fine, if that's what you want, get it. After all, you have provided well for us.' He looked so surprised and said, 'I expect the roof to cave in any minute.' I assured him it wasn't going to. Now he is talking about getting some of the things I've wanted for 17 years. But I didn't give in about the tractor to get what I wanted. I did it because I realized he truly is a good provider and deserves the things he wants."

Assignment

If your husband has not been the leader, read him the scriptures at the beginning of this chapter. Then say, "I believe these things are true, do you?" Tell him, "I want to support you as leader, for I want to become a feminine woman."

Then discuss with him some of the duties of the leader. And say, "I want to support you in the decisions which you must make." and add, "I will also support you in the plans which you might have for me and the children even though I may not always agree in principle."

If you have had the burden of finances and want to be relieved of it explain to him the principles in that section and write down the financial responsibilities of each of you. Then ask him if he agrees. If he does not, then say, "I don't think I can carry this load of complete responsibility any longer, for it is burdensome to me. I don't feel that it would be nearly as difficult for you for you are a *man*. Will you please relieve me of it?" Assure him that you will work efficiently to do your part "to make a dollar stretch" and "provide peace at home." Then when he tells you that he will do it, say, with feminine enthusiasm, "Oh, thank you, I am so glad that you will!"

CHAPTER VIII

Man the Protector

MAN'S DESIRE TO BE SUPERIOR AS PROTECTOR

When we consider the natural man, we can see that he was created to be protector of his wife and children. Man is larger, has powerful muscles, and greater physical endurance than woman. Woman, on the other hand, is delicate, fragile and weaker than man. She is like a fine precision machine which was created for the more delicate tasks and which runs smoothly and efficiently when used for the purpose intended.

Man has courage to face great dangers and difficulties of life. But women are inclined to be afraid of dangers and dread to face difficulties beyond their realm of womanhood.

Men *like* to feel brave, strong and capable, for when they do they feel their sense of manliness stirring within them. Therefore, men *enjoy* protecting women. When men become loving and romantic they often reveal this inner desire to protect woman.

John Alden revealed his desire to protect Priscilla when he said, "Here for her sake will I stay and like an invisible presence hover around her forever, protecting, supporting her weakness."

Victor Hugo made known his desire when he said, "My duty is to keep close to her steps, to surround her existence with mine, to serve as a barrier against all dangers; to offer my head as a stepping stone, to place myself unceasingly between her and all sorrows . . . if she but consent to lean upon me at times amidst the difficulties of life."

WHAT DO WOMEN NEED PROTECTION FROM?

In all periods of time women have needed protection from the dangers, strenuous work and difficulties of life. In the early history of our country the very conditions under which people were forced to live made manly protection necessary. There were dangers everywhere. Savage Indians, wild beasts and snakes created situations which called for masculine strength and ability. Such protection as men offered made them feel heroic and brave. Although our situation today is widely different, women still need protection, and offering such protection continues to make men feel heroic.

PROTECTION NEEDED TODAY

1. *Dangers.* The great danger of today is that of sexual assault and in connection with it—the threat to life itself. Most of us are aware of the tragic number of cases which have occurred. This is a *real* danger to all women and one we need to face honestly.

There are also *unreal* dangers which a truly feminine woman has and which, although they amuse man, will arouse his sense of chivalry. There are such things as lightning, thunder, and strange noises. No one denies that these are possible dangers, but they are certainly not likely. And then there are small creatures like mice and spiders that send women hopping on a chair for safety. It doesn't matter whether the danger is real or not. If the woman *thinks* it is real, she needs protection from it and man is only too anxious to give her that protection and quiet her fears.

2. *Strenuous work.* Because of her delicate physical structure woman needs protection from strenuous work. Mowing the lawn, painting the house, lifting heavy objects, moving furniture, and spading the flower beds all require more strength than the normal woman has without injury to her health and feminine charm.

3. *Difficulties of life.* In her feminine role, a woman has many difficulties which she needs to face alone. Such things as discouragements with household tasks, mistakes in household management, problems in the care of the children and disappointments in life are faced quietly and with great courage by women of real character. However, there are other difficulties of another type for which she needs masculine protection. I refer to such things as facing financial entanglements, belligerent creditors, people who have become irritable, harsh or offensive, troublesome salesmen, and people who make unreasonable demands. The feminine woman is emotional, easily upset and less capable of defending herself than man. She needs his protection!

Are Women Protected?

Are women protected from the dangers, strenuous work and difficulties of life in our present day? Let's take a look.

We see women who walk down dark streets alone. Some take long distance trips without a man present. An emergency of car trouble would place them in the presence of strange men. Some brave the storm or the dark and some kill their own spiders, mice and even their own snakes.

And are they protected from the strenuous tasks? We see women building fences, hauling sand, repairing automobiles, painting, mowing the lawn, repairing heavy equipment, fixing the roof, doing carpentry, and many other masculine tasks.

Are women protected from difficulty? Not always. Women often "go to battle!" We see them face creditors, irksome salesmen and offensive landlords. The following will illustrate:

Braving Difficulties

A man built a large market and it became a growing success. A chain grocery company built a store across the street from his and because of their competitive prices caused his market to become unprofitable. The man was so depressed that he went to bed over the matter. His wife went to the store, faced his creditors and fought the financial battles for him.

Difficulties

A couple purchased a home which was to have been vacated on a specific date. When the time arrived for occupancy the former owners refused to move. The wife faced this problem by telephoning them often but each time she was met with resistance. Finally, the former owner said, "We are going to remain here until our new home is finished and there is nothing you can do to make us move unless you take us to court." The harshness of the tenant and the trying circumstances brought the wife to tears. Her husband stayed in the background and she continued the battle until they moved.

Difficulty

Another couple planned to build a home and sought advice from a contractor concerning their houseplans. He spent many hours helping them—but when they sought bids they decided upon another contractor. Both the man and wife dreaded to face the first one and tell him their decision. It fell to the wife to face this difficulty.

Why is there this lack of chivalry? It exists because of lack of understanding.

WOMAN'S THINKING

Woman has not properly understood man. She has not realized that he enjoys protecting her. She may hesitate to lean on him for fear of imposing. On some occasions she might even refuse his chivalry. She often does things for herself thinking he will appreciate it. And he adds to her blindness by thanking her for it (but he doesn't really appreciate it). She gradually learns to do without man's care and becomes capable. Should she be surprised to find that when she really needs his chivalry he withholds it?

MAN'S THINKING

When he first married, he thought that women were supposed to be fragile and dependent upon man. But he noticed that his wife began doing many of these things for herself. Why? He didn't understand why. But she doesn't appear to be the true feminine woman that needs masculine protection. So he withholds it, because it appears unnecessary. Lack of chivalry has arisen then because:

Women have become capable which makes *manly protection unnecessary.*

WHY SHOULD WE RETURN TO CHIVALRY?

It doesn't appear that man enjoys protecting woman, for he seldom bothers to offer his services. And it does not appear that woman needs him for she appears capable "of killing her own snakes." Why not keep this situation? Why return to chivalry?

If you will investigate, you will find that neither the man nor the woman enjoys this situation, for both are robbed of an essential element of happiness. Man is robbed of his feeling of superiority and woman of her feminine charm.

WHY CHIVALRY IS ESSENTIAL

1. Protecting woman causes a man to have a thrilling realization of his manhood. He feels like the superior male.

2. If you are to become Angela Human you must become the fragile dependent creature that nature intended you to be.

You might agree that chivalry is important, *but how do you awaken it in man?*

How to Arouse Chivalry

1. By making him feel superior as your protector. Admire his superior strength and ability and the protective qualities.
2. By acquiring the quality of femininity, which is a human trait. It will be taught in chapter 14.

The object of this chapter is to concentrate on the first method. The following experience illustrates its effectiveness:

Success Story (Admiring the Manly)

The following illustrates how such chivalry can be won: A man began remodeling his wife's kitchen, but when half way completed he stopped. She tried every persuasion to get him to finish it, but she was unsuccessful.

Then she learned of this philosophy, and said: "Oh, I admire you for taking upon yourself such a *mammoth* job as remodeling this kitchen. I don't know of another man that would attempt such a job. They would call in a carpenter. You have such masculine talent." That is all she said that day.

The next day she said to her sister, (while he was within ear's distance) "Did you see what a beautiful finish my husband achieved on this cabinet door? He has a real talent working with wood." That was all she said.

The result? Within only three days he resumed the remodeling job, and very shortly completed her beautiful kitchen. It is important to understand why he stopped. It was because his wife became pushy about having it completed. He refused to continue as a means of defending his freedom. But when she stopped pushing and used the admiration approach she awakened his chivalry.

Object of this chapter: *Make him feel superior in his role as protector, and by so doing you arouse his chivalry.*

Assignment

Tell him: "I am glad that I have a man to protect me. I think it would be difficult to go through this life without you."

CHAPTER IX

Man the Provider

HIS DESIRE TO BE SUPERIOR AS PROVIDER

Since the beginning of time man has been recognized as the provider, for his first commandment was to "earn his bread by the sweat of his face," whereas woman's was to bring forth children. Since that time, man and woman's duties have been thus divided. In our present time, man is still considered the provider, for by law he is required to pay alimony as support in the event of divorce.

But man cannot be considered the sole provider today. 1964 statistics from the president's commission on the Status of Women reports that now every third worker in the American economy is a woman. By age 20, eight of ten girls will be working in paid employment or will have previously worked for pay. It is a working woman's generation.

Many working women of today are married. Can harm come as a result of the wife working? If she enjoys it and is efficient enough to manage her domestic life as well, can harm come to her or her family because of it? Many men even encourage their wives to work. If both man and wife approve the idea shouldn't she continue? Is there a valid reason for keeping the old law, "man the breadwinner?" The following are problems to consider:

HARM FROM WOMEN WORKING

1. *Children.* Most working wives are aware of the harm which can come to children, but have determined that *theirs* will not be neglected and that they *will* spend sufficient time with them. However, it is not entirely a matter of time, but of *interest.* The woman who works divides her interest from her children. She finds it difficult "to serve two masters." Her work may require that she give much of herself in effort and attention. Children

are not so demanding, and therefore are most apt to be neglected.

2. *Harm to the woman.* Also serious is the harm which may come to the *woman* who works. When she attempts to play a part not intended for her she sacrifices her own special beauty and grace. The moon, when it moves from its sphere of night into day, loses its lustre, its charm, its very poetry. And so it is with woman, when she attempts to play a part not intended for her. Gone is the lustre, the charm, the poetry that says "She is a phantom of delight."

3. *Harm to the man.* And when woman moves into man's sphere, she dims his glory and robs him of his feeling of superiority in his masculine role. One cannot over-emphasize the importance of this feeling of superiority to man's basic happiness, his ability to succeed in life, and the love he feels for his wife he is supporting and protecting.

You may agree that there are dangers in working and you might be the kind of woman that much prefers to stay home. But you might also feel that in your own case you have to work because of circumstances. But do you really? Let us examine some of the reasons why women work to see if these reasons are justified.

Reasons Why Women Work

1. *To further a man's education or advancement.* This reason is usually justifiable on the grounds that he is training himself to be a superior provider. It is, however, the way many women are introduced into the working world and some continue indefinitely.

2. *Compelling emergency.* I refer to unemployment of the man for any reason. (Not to death—since man's ego is not involved). or to distressing financial circumstances or demands. Since she must work because of the compelling emergency she has no choice in the matter and the problem to resolve is "how it can be accomplished with the least injury to her husband's pride." When she understands man's characteristics, she can help relieve this painful experience. If she will maintain a dependent attitude and regard her working as a noble sacrifice, it is better than to appear as a hero who has come to his rescue. She should let him know that she now realizes "how tough it is to be the

breadwinner—and how has he done it all these years?" This will convince him that if he were in his proper position as the breadwinner he would be much more capable than she. He will continue to feel like the superior provider.

3. *To increase the family income.* Why this need occurs:

a. Because the man's salary does not cover the necessities. But what are the necessities? They are food, clothing and shelter. Most men's salaries cover the necessities when they are defined in simple terms. Many items have been added that are not necessities—but luxuries.

b. The luxuries: Is it a new stove, boat, clothes, cabin in the mountains? Often women must work to obtain these luxuries.

c. To ease the load for the man: Women sometimes worry about their men—so they attempt to lift their burdens by working and earning part of the income. The commandment to provide the living, however, was given to *man.* Along with this, God blessed man with inherent capabilities of fulfilling this assignment. In other words, He blessed man with the necessary strength and endurance to provide for his family—if the man but seek these blessings due him. Therefore, it appears unnecessary for the woman to "ease the load" for man, but rather to encourage his strength and ability to do these things for himself.

When the woman works to increase the family income, for the three reasons I have mentioned, it is detrimental to the male ego. If he cannot provide his family with the comforts or even the neccessities of life then he does not feel like a man any longer. Or if he has to lean on his wife to lift his burdens, his ego seriously suffers. It is in this area that the most serious damage is done to the man for *he does not feel like the superior provider.*

What is the solution? The first is to cut expenses to meet the income, then she should build up her husband's self esteem so he can become an adequate provider.

4. *Because of being bored at home.* Many women work because they are bored at home. Sometimes the husband even suggests his wife work, for he can detect her boredom. Although such a reason for working does not especially affect the man's ego, it does harm the woman, for she tends to lose her womanliness. She seeks her happiness on a road where it will never be found. She

may feel a temporary relief from boredom, but she will be enjoying the weeds instead of flowers.

What about the older woman who has many hours alone at home? What can she do for fulfillment when her family is reared? Her empty hours can be spent helping the downtrodden and discouraged, for a woman's function is, *to shed joy around, and cast light upon dark days.* And although this may appear inconsistant—she possibly could become a school teacher, giving her public service in this desperately needed field. The teaching of children is not unwomanly—and will not injure the man's ego if performed with benevolent intentions.

Another suitable field for the older woman is that of nursing, an occupation which has always been considered feminine and benevolent. But whatever the job the older woman seeks, it is the *motive for working* and her *femininity* which are important to consider. If her reason is benevolence, a desire to fill the empty hours with service to humanity, and if the service be of a feminine nature, her motive becomes a noble sacrifice and one which will glorify her womanhood rather than degrade it.

Mistakes the "Stay at Home " Wife Makes

The working wife is not the only one that crushes the man's ego? The one who stays home makes such remarks as "We can't afford it," or "I wish we had a little more security." She may offer suggestions about how he may increase his income. Or she may admire another man who has been financially successful. Even calling attention to her thrift may affect him adversely—knowing that his wife must "scrimp" to make his salary do. All of these things make a man feel like an "inferior" provider. The following dialogue illustrates this loss of esteem:

Tom: As he looks over his bills, "It takes a lot of money to support a family now days." (hoping for praise)

Mary: "Well, it's not my fault! I scrimp and save and sew and mend. I make the children's clothes, make our bread, and never buy luxuries for myself. Other women go to the beauty salon to have their hair done, but not me!" (hoping to win appreciation)

Tom: "Do you really go without?" (hoping she will reassure him)

Mary: "I am only trying to help. A woman's supposed to

help share her husband's burdens. I would rather go without the things I need than to see you worry." (hoping again for appreciation)

Tom: (something inside of him happens. It is a mixture of resentment towards her for making him feel like a failure and a miserable feeling of being one.) He says with irritation, "Guess I'm not much of a provider in your eyes, am I?" (Mary looks up in bewilderment at his irritation and lack of appreciation for her self sacrifice.)

The above is a perfect illustration of the lack of understanding between the sexes. The only reason Tom complained of the high costs was to win Mary's appreciation. But she took it as criticism. And her defense—the scrimping wife—was a blow to his ego.

The following dialogue is an illustration of what she should have said:

The Right Way

Tom: "It takes a lot of money to support a family now days."

Mary: "Doesn't it though. I guess we're pretty extravagant aren't we? How have you managed so well with such a spendthrift wife! (Although she isn't one, of course.) Isn't it a tremendous responsibility to be a man and have to provide for a family? I'm glad I'm not a man—I would bend under the load, I'm afraid."

Tom: (his self esteem has doubled) "Well, now, I don't mind the load at all. Of course, it does have its trying problems. But I feel capable of the job! Yes—quite capable!!"

Mary: "It is wonderful to feel secure and to know that I have a man that will always provide for me!"

In the first illustration, Mary made her husband feel like a failure, but in the second—*like a hero.*

Assignment

Tell him: "I'm happy that you take such good care of me, and that you provide me with the *comforts* of life. Is it a load? (let him explain) How do you bear the responsibility? I'm glad I'm not a man—it would be tough for me."

In this way, you help him feel superior in his role.

Six Rules for Making Him Feel Superior in His Role

1. *Reverence his position* as leader, protector, and provider, and defend his authority before his children.

2. *Admire his superior strength and masculine ability,* and tell him that you do.

3. *Do not excel him* in anything which requires masculine strength or ability.

4. *Be dependent.* Demonstrate your dependency if you are called upon to take masculine responsibility.

5. *Have a girlish trust in him.* Never doubt his ability to take care of you, to provide for you and guide you safely through life.

6. *Be feminine.* When you appear as a woman he will feel like a man.

The last three rules are human qualities and will be explained in that part of the book.

CHAPTER X

Make Him No. 1

A man wants a woman who will place him at the top of her priority list—not second, but first. He wants to be the king-pin around which all other activities of her life revolve. He does not want to be the background music to her other interests and dreams.

Do women give their men this honor? Few of them do! For other things take precedence, such as the following:

1. *The children.* For example: A woman was the mother of a large family. Everyone who knew her admired her as the model mother. But her husband appeared to be only an appendage. The center of her life was her children. She lived and breathed for them. She loved and appreciated her husband and treated him well enough, but he never received top priority. His role was father and provider—but not king! What was the result?

When he was alone with his wife, he was kind and affectionate, and when alone with the children he enjoyed their companionship. But when they were together he had a resentful attitude towards both of them. He criticized and belittled his children and resented his wife for placing him in this inferior position.

This inferior position causes men to resent the birth of a new baby. And it accounts for a frequent attitude of refusal to have more children.

Placing her husband No. 1 in her life does not diminish the sacred responsibility a woman has for her children, nor is it an indication of lesser love for them. Actually, the children feel more secure in the mothers love and interest when she shows such honor to her leader.

2. *Homemaking.* Sometimes it is her home that becomes more important to the woman than the man himself. Homemaking tasks, sewing, redecorating or dreams of new furniture may dom-

inate her thinking or time. But is the castle more important than the king who dwells therein?

3. *Appearance.* When it comes to appearance, a man appreciates a well groomed, well dressed wife when the effort is made for his sake. But if she spends endless hours shopping, sewing and grooming, and in so doing neglects him, it gives him the impression that it is others she is trying to impress. He does not feel that he is No. 1 in her life.

4. *Money and security.* Occasionally a woman will resist the decision of her husband when such a decision would threaten her security. She may discourage an investment, change of occupation, further education or other plans for the future which she feels would or could impair the security she has now. She is saying, in effect, your money, or what you are providing for me now is more important than you—than your fulfillment or challenges which you as a man feel you would like to meet.

Not only does she place emphasis on the material things above the man himself, but her attitude would suggest that she is afraid he will fail, which is a severe blow to one of man's most vulnerable characteristics—his pride. In her resistance to his plans she places money and security ahead of the man, his feelings, his experiences, his pride and his confidence in himself.

A woman told me of an incident in her life in which she made such a choice. Her husband wanted to expand his business and in so doing planned to move the family into a small apartment temporarily, to sell the family home and use the money for his business expansion. But the wife "put her foot down" and refused to move. She said, "I did not mind the inconvenience, for I have lived in lesser circumstances." Her reason was that she was afraid her husband would fail. She chose security at a risk of his feelings, his pride and his self-confidence.

At other times, a woman's desire for money and security may be the underlying reason why she may *push* him towards a goal he may resist. Security becomes more important than the man, than his freedom to be himself, and to be the leader. Her attitude also suggests to him that she is dissatisfied with their present economic status, and such a suggestion is a serious threat to his pride.

For example, a girl of my aquaintance is married to a man of rather lowly economic status. For a number of years she has suggested to him that he study to become a medical doctor. Her attitude suggests to him that she is not satisfied with his income, and perhaps his lack of prestige. If she continues to encourage him to become a doctor, she is placing money and prestige ahead of the man himself.

5. *The wife's parents.* When a wife feels a strong love and attachment for her parents, which exceeds the feelings she has for her husband, it naturally causes him to feel that he is not No. 1 in her life. This, in turn, may cause him to resent his wife's parents, for they may steal from his position of importance.

6. *Careers, talents and other activities.* Most men would like to extend to their wives the freedom to develop talents and to engage in activities which they may enjoy, but when these interests dominate the woman's thinking, and when her enthusiasm for them overshadows the man himself, it causes him to feel second place to her other interests. This is the reason men often become quite unreasonable about the time their wives spend away from domestic life, and even refuse to allow them these privileges.

If, however, the woman places her husband No. 1 in her life, he is likely to encourage her interest in outside activities, since it does not appear as a competition to him.

Often men who are "second fiddle" leave their wives and seek women who make them feel of prime importance. It is seldom sex that drives a man to a mistress. It is her ability to make him feel like a king, as in the following experience as related to me:

How I Encouraged My Husband to Have Other Women

Sounds terrible doesn't it? And it was, and now after studying and practicing Fascinating Womanhood, I am beginning to realize that all his escapades were brought on by my behavior towards him, and that's why I say *"I."*

This is how it happened: Our sex life was good, the only good part of our marriage, it seemed. I told my husband so and complimented him on being such a wonderful lover, but the trouble was, that was the only thing I complimented him for or admired him for. I found nothing to praise him in; I certainly didn't accept him; he was never treated as Number 1. In other words, I counted him as good for nothing except a sex partner. Therefore, he turned to other women who made him feel Number 1, and admired his other manly attributes; he turned to women who would listen to his stories and give him the time and the attention every man needs. Of course I hated him for having other women. I couldn't understand why he wasn't satisfied with the sex I gave him. After Fascinating Womanhood, I saw that it wasn't the sex he needed from these other women, but acceptance and admiration, and that by withholding these things from him, I had driven him to unfaithfulness.

I have no fears now that he will ever have another escapade, because I now know what kind of woman a man wants.

Should He Place You No. 1 in Importance?

Man's first obligation in life is to *provide* for his wife and children. He knows that he must work to eat and that occasionally he may have to neglect his wife and children to do so. From a practical standpoint it is impossible to place her first, and she has no right to expect it.

He may put her first in his heart if she is Angela Human, but he will have to make her second place to providing for his family.

The Lord told woman that man was to *rule over her.* And the Apostle Paul said *reverence your husbands.* Doesn't this imply that she should give him the homage due a king? And doesn't this make him No. 1?

Conclusions—Understanding Men

We have come to the end of the section "Understanding Man." This is the Angelic quality which Agnes had in such abundance which brought David peace and happiness. And when he did not have her understanding he "seemed to go wild and to get into difficulty."

Understanding men is an angelic quality, and therefore is a matter of character. Our lack of understanding indicates the weakness in our character. Trampling on his freedom, lack of humility, lack of sympathy and forgiveness, our failure to see his better side and our unwillingness to cast out the beam from our own eye are at the root of many of our mistakes. Even our lack of knowledge shows our weakness. Have we pleaded to the Lord to give us light and understanding when in darkness? Have we been too content to enjoy weeds instead of flowers?

The rewards which can come into a marriage as a result of "understanding men" knows no bounds. As one wife put it, "Our marriage blossomed like a plant that had been placed in the sun after a long, dark winter." This is due to the love and tenderness that is awakened in a man's heart when he feels accepted, free, respected as a man and understood. Such a display of tenderness is impressive in the following experience:

SUCCESS STORY

My husband and I have been married 6 years—we have 2 children. When I became pregnant with my last child my husband became very cold and indifferent. He said he didn't love me and said I was like a mother to him. He began having an affair with another woman. After the baby was born, I filed for divorce and we got a settlement and separated. But my husband didn't want a divorce. We went to a marriage counselor for help and he told us what was wrong but didn't tell us how to make things right. After being separated for three months we went back together on a six months trial. We were both miserable separated. We were from very religious homes and attended and were very active in our own church when this happened.

During this trial period our marriage was doing fairly well, but was shakey and wasn't what I wanted. I didn't feel the tenderness I wanted and needed so desperately. I didn't feel loved like I wanted to be. I felt like our marriage was very insecure but I didn't know what to do about it. I felt helpless and worried constantly that my husband would find another woman to have an affair with.

At this time I heard about Fascinating Womanhood. I read the book and attended the classes. The first time I practiced it, I saw my husband's face light up and felt a tenderness, though small, towards me. We had had very little communication but when I started *admiring him* and giving him the *sympathetic understanding* that you describe he became a changed man. His shell has disappeared and he tells me all his problems and treats me with a lovely tender feeling. It is a marvelous experience—one I have always dreamed of but never had. The more I admire him the more love I feel from him.

I now have a wonderful peace within. I have no fear of him leaving me for another woman because I am giving him the admiration and love he needs and wants and in turn I receive the love I so desperately need.

PANDORA'S BOX

When a marriage has had real problems, and then the woman makes a particular effort to improve it by applying the principles of Fascinating Womanhood, it often causes a peculiar reaction in her husband known as Pandora's Box.

In this case, when Fascinating Womanhood is applied, instead of the man being loving and tender, it may cause him to become extremely violent and appear to be hateful towards his wife.

It is important to understand the change which is taking place within the man which causes this violent outburst. For years he may have suppressed hateful feelings towards his wife, for fear he might bring on a marriage failure. If he is a high principled man and loves his children, he has probably made great effort to hold his marriage securely together. In order to do this he has had to suppress feelings of hate and resentment towards his wife.

When she applies Fascinating Womanhood for a period of time he gradually begins to feel *secure* in his marriage. Then, at last he dares to open Pandora's Box and let all of the hateful feelings that have been hiding there escape.

It is important for the wife to understand this reaction and allow him to empty Pandora's Box. Agree with him, and encourage him to express himself. When the last hateful feeling has escaped and the box is empty, he will have a feeling of love and tenderness towards her not known before, and his reserve may completely disappear, as in the following experiences:

SUCCESS STORY (Pandora's Box)

After learning and applying Fascinating Womanhood, my husband seemed happier, but that lasted only about 3 to 4 months, when tension began to build a little. (not bad). Then one evening, wham! A Pandora's Box reaction. It seems as if all the pent up feelings he had came out and at the same time the walls of reserve came tumbling down. Pretty dramatic—and pretty wonderful! Now he tells me he has never been so happy in all his life and I feel the same way. Even friends comment on it and ask if I am really as happy as I look.

I really feel the spirit of Fascinating Womanhood and the deep happiness it can bring when one lives it. Tonight my husband spent three hours just talking to me, telling me more about himself, his past and dreams than I have learned in ten years of marriage. He also said that he came closer than I had realized to leaving me during that time and would have if it hadn't been for the children.

SUCCESS STORY (Pandora's Box)

I had been extremely happy all day, but when my husband came home he cast a shadow of gloom and was grumpy. I was determined to not let his gloom rub off on me. I made him comfortable and invited him to talk over the day. He just wanted to relax so I continued to prepare dinner.

When I went to call him to dinner, his head was bowed and wet tears were on his cheeks. Tenderly, I softly said, "Dear, share it with me." All of sudden he burst into deep sobs, and he opened the lid of Pandora's Box. He had lost all faith in womanhood through the tragic experience of a previous marriage. Out stormed all of his resentments, hatred towards women and fears of the future. He had opened his shell. Since that evening, our love has had the freedom to grow, even to the height of him telling me with a big hug that I am everything a man could want in a wife.

CHAPTER XI

Deep Inner Happiness

Above all, a man wants a woman who is genuinely happy. If her eyes reveal that she is upset, disturbed or unhappy, it may arouse his sympathy, but it will not arouse his admiration and love. If we would acquire inner happiness we must understand what it is and where it is found.

WHAT IS IT?

Inner happiness is a feeling of spiritual contentment which carries one through the triumphs, pitfalls or even heartaches of life with equally calm stability. It is serenity, peace of mind and tranquility. Agnes possessed inner happiness, for she had "a placid and sweet expression" and "a tranquility about her—a quiet, good calm spirit."

HAPPINESS VERSUS PLEASURE

Everyone wants this inner peace, but how many actually find it? The trouble with many of us is that we seek happiness on the wrong road. We seek it on the road to pleasure. Often we think that if we just had the home of our dreams or some new furniture, carpeting, or a charming wardrobe, then we would be happy. Or we may feel that if we could live in a particular community, or have money for the comforts or pleasures of life, then we could be happy. These things do of course have a certain value, but they are not the requirements for inner happiness. There are women who have none of these material things and they enjoy inner peace. On the other hand, some who have them all are miserable.

There are, of course, good and bad pleasures. The pleasures which come from sin should be avoided completely. But the good pleasures can enrich life if added to the foundation of inner happiness. Good pleasures are such things as sunshine, rain, and flowers, nourishing food, the laughter of children, wholesome recreation, music, the arts, and many more of the finer things of life, while bad pleasures are those things which are destructive to body and spirit.

Happiness is quite different from pleasure. It often arises from a different source. Pleasure seems to come from those things which please our senses, while happiness may even arise from unpleasant experiences such as pain in childbirth, or the weariness, pain and toil by a father to secure comforts for his loved ones. Pleasure may be derived from sin while happiness is a direct result of the struggle to overcome sin. Sometimes happiness comes as a result of knowing misery, sorrow, pain and suffering.

"It will arise from a consciousness of moral, spiritual and physical strength; of strength gained in conflict; the strength that comes from experience; from having sounded the depths of the soul; from experiencing all emotions of which the mind is susceptible; from testing all the qualities and strength of the intellect." (B. H. Roberts)

No person who lives a mere innocent life, protected from experiences both good and bad can know what real joy and happiness is. How can this inner happiness be acquired? What conscious effort must we make to achieve it?

How Do We Acquire It?

You may have heard the statement "We are about as happy as we make up our minds to be." Although there is some merit in the positive outlook, the statement is not entirely correct. A wicked person cannot acquire happiness through this self deception. You cannot acquire inner happiness by determination alone but must lay the proper groundwork by living righteous principles.

Happiness is based upon eternal laws. If we are not at peace within it is because we are not obeying principles upon which this inner peace is based. Inner happiness is available to everyone and is acquired by understanding and applying its principles.

Our Greatest Source of Happiness

Our greatest source of happiness comes from the development of the spirit. The way to happiness for a woman is in the perfection of all of the Angelic Qualities. Her understanding of men will bring her great inner joy. Her successful fulfillment of her role as mother, domestic goddess and loving wife will further add to her joy. And the total development of her character will bring her a tranquil peace.

Inner happiness is not a voluntary quality which can be put on as a smile but must be earned by personal victory over our weaknesses and an upward reach for perfection.

Love Not Necessary

If you are a woman who feels unloved, you might be inclined to think, "If my husband really loved me, then I would experience inner happiness." Although love is essential to our total happiness in the highest sense, it is not essential in acquiring the inner happiness of which I speak.

Inner happiness is independent of others and outside circumstances. Not even the love of your man is required for its attainment. In fact, *you must first find inner peace before you can be loved.* I know of at least two men on the brink of divorce who commented to me that they would not consider a reconcilliation if the wife did not achieve happiness within herself. Agnes possessed inner happiness although she did not possess David's love.

Inner happiness is a personal victory, entirely within the realm of possibility for every woman. And it is charming to men.

But Inner Happiness Not Complete

Although a woman may acquire inner happiness without the love of her husband, it is not a complete happiness. Her husband's Celestial love for her is necessary for her to experience real joy and happiness. David Copperfield noticed frequently an unhappy expression in Agnes' beautiful face, but he did not realize that it was due to unrequited love. It was an indication of a missing ingredient to happiness, *but it did not detract from her tranquility of spirit.*

The Unhappy Woman

There is a dullness to the eyes that is tragic in the unhappy woman. With some there is a shuffling of the walk, poor posture, careless and lackadaisical manner and even a whine in the voice. The entire bearing of some women suggest unhappiness.

Complaining, harshness and quick judgment and negative attitudes are some of the outer signs. They have a tendency to appear older; they lose their sparkle; and there is a noticeable inner turmoil. The effect is depressing. All of these traits destroy the charm of the woman and make her unattractive to men. A man may be aroused to sympathy for an unhappy woman, but he will not feel a tender holy feeling of love and adoration for her.

THE HAPPY WOMAN

The woman who possesses inner happiness is quite the opposite. There is an inner radiance to the eyes. There will be a dignity about her bearing—an optimism, hope and faith in her attitude. She smiles easily, and suggests a feeling of contentment. She is slow to criticize. She is trustful and patient, and her spirit radiates tranquility, serenity and peace. Her appearance and influence are uplifting. She is charming to men.

STEPS TO INNER HAPPINESS

1. Understanding Men
2. Development of the Character
3. Fulfilling her role as woman—The Domestic Goddess.

I have said that the greatest source of happiness comes from the development of the spirit, and that for a woman this means the perfection of her angelic side. As she gains a greater understanding of men she will acquire the virtues of sympathy, understanding, appreciation, and gain the Christian virtue of looking to herself for failings rather than to her husband and others.

In the next chapter I have explained the importance of the total character development and stressed some of the most essential womanly virtues which enrich her life and in turn bring her inner peace.

Equally essential to her inner happiness is her faithful performance of her role as woman. Being a loving and understanding wife, a wonderful mother and a devoted and successful homemaker are key requirements to her happiness. Success in the feminine role is her real glory, and brings her an inner peace and satisfaction that cannot be met otherwise. It is impossible for the woman who neglects these sacred duties to experience real joy. She may gain satisfaction from activities and success elsewhere, but they cannot compensate for her failure as a woman. "There is no success in life to compensate for a failure in the home." (David O. McKay)

I have explained that there are laws upon which happiness is based. The three mentioned above are those involved in a woman's happiness. Violation of these laws results in her frustration and unhappiness, whereas successful performance brings her in harmony with the laws of life and offers her fulfillment and inner happiness.

Two Essential Virtues to Woman's Happiness

The development of the entire character is important, but there are two virtues which are particularly essential to woman's happiness. They are the following:

1. *Acceptance of ourselves*: In the process of becoming Angels, we are still human beings. We make mistakes and often our blunders rob us of happiness. It can be a cause of misery to a woman to make mistakes, such as burning food, making a poor purchase, or breaking an expensive object. Even the small things tend to disturb us emotionally. This is due to our failure to accept ourselves.

We must accept ourselves as we do our husbands and allow for our own weaknesses and mistakes. It is wrong to expect perfect performance of ourselves.

I read of a man who loved to travel. Sometimes he was unfairly charged by deceitful people in foreign lands. It was disturbing and took the joy out of travel to a degree. Through analysis of his problem he developed the idea of setting aside some money for each trip "to be robbed of." After such an allowance he was able to enjoy his trips.

The business man allows in advance for business failures or emergencies. We should allow for some mistakes as well. Tell yourself that each year, each week and even each day you will make your share of mistakes or unwise decisions. When you plan a wardrobe remember that you may not choose wisely with every item. In this life we learn by experience, and that experience includes its share of mistakes.

Acceptance of ourselves, however, *does not mean contentment*. It does not mean that we accept ourselves as foolish, unwise, weak or inferior human beings, making no effort to improve ourselves. Such an attitude is an enemy to progress.

It *does* mean that we accept ourselves as human, prone to make mistakes, miscalculations and use poor judgment, and although we do make great effort to improve, we will occasionally try and fail.

In our efforts to improve ourselves, we should not become discouraged and lose heart if old habits are difficult to break. In the swim upstream we are occasionally pushed back by a wave or opposing current. But this is our road to perfection.

2. *Appreciation of the simple pleasures of life*: Another virtue essential to happiness is an appreciation of the simple joys of life such as rain, sunlight or fresh crisp curtains. It is not so much these simple pleasures themselves that contribute so much to a woman's happiness as it is her ability to *appreciate* them.

The appreciative woman will enjoy drinking water from a tin cup while another feels she must have china dishes. One woman will enjoy sitting on an apple box in her backyard letting the warm summer sun shine down upon her shoulders. Another may feel she must have patio furniture to be happy. One will enjoy the sounds of the forest or the birds and the leaves rustling while another must have grand opera. One will enjoy a simple wardrobe of cottons while another lives for the day she can buy her clothes on Fifth Avenue. One feels real joy in pushing her baby buggy in the park, while another must have the bright lights and gay places. One will enjoy the simple cottage, while another must have a modern home with a view.

Little children have this ability to enjoy simple pleasures. A ray of sunshine, a tub of water to splash in are common things they enjoy. Women who learn to enjoy these common things are never left wanting.

The development of the angelic side of woman is the road to inner happiness. If you do not have happiness now, it is largely due to some weakness in your character and not to outside circumstances.

Inner happiness is an upward climb. It is like swimming upstream and is found in the great efforts and achievements of life. It is a result of the struggle to overcome evil or moral weakness, and continued effort to perfection of the spirit.

CHAPTER XII

A Worthy Character

A man wants a woman he can place on a pedestal and worship from below. He expects her to be kinder, more patient and understanding than he is and rather considers himself the more unrefined creature of the human race.

If a man becomes thoughtless, harsh or critical, he may be willing to overlook it in himself, but is disappointed to see woman—the angelic creature of the earth—fall onto his level.

He may at times shake her pedestal by suggesting some unrighteous act. He does this deliberately to see if she will remain in her high position. What a disappointment it is if she falls in character, and what a joy if she remains unshaken. Remaining on top when she is tested is further proof that she belongs there.

Before man will place woman on a pedestal, she must develop a character worthy of that position. Your first impression might be: "This is not too essential for me to know. I have been trained all my life in the development of the virtues. *I have a worthy character!* The other things in this book are of far more value to me. I am honest, kind and benevolent. You see, I have a fine character."

Such a statement indicates one's failure to understand what good character includes. The virtues mentioned above are essential, of course, but the attainment of a worthy character includes much more. Dora was kind, honest and benevolent, but she did not earn the worshipful love of David Copperfield. Few women earn the eminence of the pedestal!

There are many virtues of character—all worth every effort to acquire. The following, however, are ten of the most essential. Several of these are particularly important to women.

QUALITIES OF CHARACTER ESSENTIAL TO THE PEDESTAL

1. *Self Mastery.*
    "He who rules within himself and rules his passions, desires and fears is more than a king."

Self mastery is the foundation of a worthy character. We cannot even apply the knowledge which is in this book if we do not have the will to apply. We indicate a lack of self mastery in our failure to remain on a diet, our "unbridled tongues," our inability to keep confidences, failure to be prompt, and the failure to fulfill responsibilities. Any failure to apply principles of our conviction indicates lack of self mastery. Our fears, doubts and passions and even our goals we conquer through self mastery.

So important is self mastery to spiritual achievement that the greatest person of all time felt a need for it. Jesus Christ did not even begin his ministry until He first went into the wilderness and fasted for forty days and forty nights. During this time He gained spiritual strength and was able to endure severe temptations.

There are numerous ways of gaining self mastery. One of the most useful is the example set by the Savior, that of fasting. By depriving ourselves of food for a period of time we gain a self control that strengthens one for the challenges of life. Usually a 24-hour fast is beneficial and all that many people can endure to begin with.

There are other things which help to strengthen self control. Many philosophers have advised that we "do things which are difficult, and that we do them regularly." Taking cold showers, doing irksome tasks, demanding definite quotas of ourselves are some of the things which strengthen our self mastery so that when severe temptations come we will have fortified ourselves to resist them. Or if it is a goal which we are trying to reach, we have gained the self discipline necessary for its attainment.

2. *Unselfishness*: Regard for others—for their happiness, their success and comfort indicates an unselfish person.

> "Bear ye one another's burdens and so fulfill the law of Christ." (Gal. 6:2.)

Women especially are inclined to be self-centered and think in terms of "my children, my husband's success, my house, my wardrobe." Even our special problems dominate our thinking.

We often fail to realize what narrow selfish lives we live. I knew a couple who had no children. They spent most of their time at home working in their beautiful garden. It was lovely. One day they sold their lovely home and surroundings and moved into an apartment. They felt bored and unhappy and felt there was nothing to occupy their time. So they bought another home, planted another garden and became content.

Their self centered attitude indicates a lack of interest in others—a failure to realize the needs of those around them. Although they were honest, good neighbors, and good citizens, they were living a selfish life.

3. *Benevolence*: What is benevolence? Does it consist of taking a hot bowl of soup to Mrs. Smith who is ill, or making clothes for the poor. It is doubtful these kindnesses do any great good, for unless they are given in secret they heap an unhealthy obligation on the head of the receiver.

The greatest good comes from lifting a person's spirit and giving hope and purpose to their lives. Some need only a word of encouragement, or approval, but still others are desperate.

Those in need of help often show it in their eyes. Young people who are discouraged look downcast. True benevolence is to seek out the downcast and discouraged and restore their souls.

Give your material gifts in secret, but *lift men's spirits with the strength of your soul.*

4. *Moral Courage*: Often it is a lack of moral courage that causes us to fail to follow our convictions. Fear of ridicule, fear of criticism keep us from reaching our goals. For example: We may determine in our minds that we want to spend a great amount of time with our children. But outside influences interfere. We let others tell us how to spend our time because we do not have the moral courage to say "No."

You may have a day of housecleaning planned at home. Then someone calls you on the telephone and occupies your time. The fear of offending keeps you from indicating your boredom. And thus your life runs you instead of you running it.

5. *Patience*: There are four ways we need patience:

a. *Patience with people*: There is no better place for learning patience than in the home. The baby that cries in the night, the quarrels, confusion and misbehavior of little children give us a wonderful field for acquiring this virtue. Even people outside the home try us. True patience is not merely an act of self control but a willingness to overlook the mistakes of others.

b. *Patience with tasks*: Some women complain bitterly about their endless tasks at home—three meals a day, washing and never ending housecleaning become tiresome. But the truly feminine woman accepts these tasks with patience. How quickly will she lose her charm with an impatient attitude. The woman who can smile through her endless tasks is the one men admire.

c. *Patience with desires*: It requires patience to wait and to work for the fulfillment of our goals. It may be a new home, remodeling the old one, new furniture, or time to develop talents that you desire. Some women become impatient, and fill their desires at the expense of others. Often it is the husband who must meet the impatient demands of his wife who "wants it now." Or if she doesn't have her wish she may become embittered or complaining.

It will require patience to apply the principles of Fascinating Womanhood and reap the rewards in store.

d. *Patience to look for the brighter day*: We all have our disappointments and sorrows, but "How poor are they who have not patience to wait." (Shakespeare) The patient willingness to begin anew is a sign of character.

We can learn patience by watching nature in her methods of reaching her objectives. If you will take a trip to a limestone cave you will see the beautiful patterns built by drops of water falling from the ceiling. It takes centuries to produce this beauty.

6. *Chastity*: I refer to sexual purity of act and thought. There is a relaxing of moral standards in our present time even among those who profess Christianity. An acceptance of sexual sin and even "free love" in marriage exists. But a woman cannot arouse a man's Celestial love if she is not chaste. Her husband may have a passion for her, but it will not be genuine love.

Women are often unchaste in appearance and often invite sensual desire in men other than their husbands by their immodest clothes, their loose actions and mannerisms, their coy glances, their extreme makeup and by their flattery.

Then there is the jesting among married couples that would imply immoral acts and it is passed off as humor. Such statements as "Your son looks like the milkman" suggest immorality. Sexual immorality destroys the spirit, personality and beauty of the woman. She is certainly not our ideal of Angela Human.

7. *Honesty*: Few of us would steal or bear false witness, or tell obvious lies, but there are common ways that we fall into dishonesty. It is usually for one of two reasons:

a. *Fear of criticism or disapproval*: This fault is as old as our mother, Eve, for when accused of taking the forbidden fruit, she offered this excuse, "The serpent beguiled me" rather than to face the wrath of God. How often we will offer some excuse rather than to face the disapproval of our husbands. When late for an appointment due to our own laziness we may say, "The children detained me," or when we fail to have meals on time or our house clean we might complain that we didn't feel well.

b. *Money—the root of our dishonesty*. There are women who will lie about a child's age to save fare on a train, or in a movie or the circus. It is common to return items to a store on the grounds of improper fit or defect when the real reason is a change of mind. How many would buy items wholesale by deceptive means? There are those who will accidentally damage a parked automobile and fail to leave identification. The woman worthy of the pedestal need keep her honesty "in trim."

8. *Humility*: There are three ways we need have humility.

a. *With worldly goods*: In the book of Proverbs the Lord mentions seven things which He hates, and the first on the list is *"A Proud Look."* It is difficult for those who have money and possessions to keep from being proud. There is a natural tendency for women who are dressed in expensive and stylish clothes and drive the latest model automobile and live in luxurious surroundings to feel superior to those women who have less. In some cases they even delight in making those without material wealth feel inferior by parading their fine possessions before those they consider their inferiors. Such lack of humility indicates spiritual weakness.

b. *With knowledge*: Higher education, native ability, gifts and talents, and what some consider higher intelligence cause some women to be lifted up in pride. They may feel that this is only honest arrogance or self realization. How can they feel humble when they realize this greater ability? The proper attitude is the awareness of the greater sea of knowledge yet undiscovered—the greater gifts and talents of others now living and those who have lived on before. This thought places a person in his proper position of humility.

c. *Righteousness*: We have learned already of woman's self righteous attitude which causes her to become critical of her husband and try to improve him. Even the attainment of a worthy character and climbing to the position of the pedestal should not cause a woman to feel superior in righteousness. "And whosoever shall exalt himself shall be abased; and he that shall humble himself shall be exalted." There is always someone to whom you can compare yourself that is more worthy. There is always some greater nobility which we can be striving to attain.

9. *Self dignity*: There is an element of character which makes a woman queenly and it is called self dignity. When she has this virtue she commands the respect of all around her. She may be unselfish, humble, yielding and obedient, but she maintains an attitude of respect for herself which others can detect and admire. This quality can best be understood by observing those who lack it, as in the following situations:

There are those women who lack self-dignity by being *too servile*. They wait upon their families from morning until night and are not mothers and wives, but slaves. No request is too great or too small. In their efforts to serve their families they disregard their own needs as human beings. They do not command the respect of a queen, but reduce themselves in the eyes of their family to that of *drudge*. Instead of being appreciated for their efforts, they only succeed in arousing a feeling of disrespect and even contempt.

If, on the other hand, the woman maintains her self dignity and has a personal regard for her own worth and needs, her efforts to care for her family become a noble sacrifice and she is admired for it.

Also lacking in self dignity is the woman who strives *valiantly to please her husband*, while neglecting her own personal needs. She may cater to his every whim and desire, save her nickels and dimes for special luxuries for him, always remembers his birthday (while he usually forgets hers) and approves of his luxurious spending and indulgences. At the same time she goes without things she needs. Such actions would seem to a man a trait of character, but when the effort to please him is made at her own expense, instead of arousing appreciation, it causes him to lose respect for her. He likes being made comfortable and enjoys her thoughtfulness, but he does not like her lack of regard for herself as a person. She thinks too much of him and too little of herself. She has spoiled him, when a better relationship exists when the husband spoils the wife.

Still another way a woman can lack self dignity is in allowing her husband to *mistreat her*. We need to allow for man's small offenses, but when the man is extremely thoughtless, insulting or unfair, his wife should defend herself. A man does not admire a woman he can "walk on." He admires the woman who has the self dignity and spunk to express herself. If she does not respect herself as a human being, will allow herself to be treated unkindly, then it is difficult for her husband to respect her properly. Rising to a spirit of self dignity when she has been mistreated can be charming to a man and he loves her more deeply because of it. How to respond to such mistreatment will be taught in chapter 18.

When the woman is too servile, too willing to please and will allow mistreatment, or when she in any way appears in an inferior position to her husband, she does not have the queenly quality of self dignity.

10. *The gentle tender quality*: There is a quality of character which is vital to our ideal of Angela Human—and it is tenderness and gentleness. This is a quality which is a combination of several virtues, such as sympathy, benevolence, understanding, compassion, patience, long suffering, and kindness.

This quality is an attractive feminine quality of character which you display to others through your feminine manner. It is difficult, if not impossible, for a woman to be truly feminine without this character trait, for if she is harsh, critical, or bitter, feminine charm is destroyed.

THE WOMAN OF WEAK CHARACTER

Women who are weak in character lose their charm. They may have perfect physical features, yet there will be a hard expression about the mouth, a coldness to the eyes, or an irritation on the otherwise fair forehead and a droop to the shoulders that spoil their beauty. The shadowy hint of an unworthy character will mar the beauty of an otherwise perfect face.

THE WOMAN WITH A WORTHY CHARACTER

The beauty and tranquility that a woman acquires with the

attainment of a worthy character makes her attractive to men. There will be a softness about the face and in the eyes and a calmness in the voice and the manner that is appealing. *"Beauty is the mark God set on virtue!"*

IF YOU DO NOT HAVE A WORTHY CHARACTER

Do not become discouraged and think that attaining a worthy character is beyond your possibility. If you have lived a weak and selfish life, you can start living a clean and righteous one. We all have Angelic potential and it is never too late.

Mahatma Gandhi was weak and worldly as a young man. But he had such tremendous spiritual growth that he is known today as the "Great Soul." An integral part of his philosophy of life is the possibility of ordinary people becoming great souls in this lifetime. He proved this by his own example.

> Trust in thine own untried capacity,
> As thou would trust in God Himself.
> Thy soul is but an emanation from the whole.
> Thou dost not dream what forces lie in thee,
> Vast and unfathomed as the boundless sea.
> (Author Unknown)

HOW TO CONVINCE HIM THAT
YOU BELONG ON THE PEDESTAL

1. *Let your light shine*: Do not put your angelic character under a bushel where he cannot see it. Do some good works so that he can see the light of your soul.

2. *Appreciate his spiritual qualities*: If you want to prove to him that you have strength of character, then appreciate the noble character in him. If you appreciate his honesty, dependability and fairness, you only prove that you claim these attributes as your own.

3. *Appreciate the character in others*: If you appreciate Mrs. Jones only because she has a nice hairdo or Mr. Smith because his place of business is nicely decorated, it does little to display character to your husband. But if you recognize their unselfishness, their benevolence and their patience, you prove that you have fine character, for you are so quick to perceive it in others. And if you are back biting and faultfinding in others—you will fall off your pedestal!

If you want to be on a pedestal, you must acquire a character worthy of that position.

CHAPTER XIII

The Domestic Goddess

The term "Domestic Goddess" implies something more than a clean, orderly home, well behaved children and delicious meals. It relates to the woman herself, indicating a glory which she has added to the home which causes her to appear as a goddess. In other words, a woman may achieve success as a homemaker and yet fail to be a goddess. This is due to her failure to see herself as the central figure in the home with a personality which radiates to others.

The Domestic Goddess must, of course, be successful as a homemaker, but beyond this accomplishment she adds a light warmth and spirit to the home which adds a special quality to her calling as a homemaker.

The quality of the Domestic Goddess is found in our studies of Agnes, Amelia and Deruchette. Agnes was as "staid and discreet a housekeeper as the old house could have." Amelia was a "kind, smiling, tender little domestic goddess whom men are inclined to worship."

Deruchette's "presence lights the home; her approach is like a cheerful warmth; she passes by and we are content; she stays awhile and we are happy. . . . Her occupation was only to live her daily life." Hugo also compares her to a little bird, "a bird transmuted into a young maiden; what could be more exquisite? Picture it in your home and call it Deruchette. . . .

"The wings are invisible but the chirping may still be heard. Sometimes too she pipes a clear, loud song. . . . She flits from branch to branch, or rather from room to room; goes to and fro; approaches and returns; plumes her wings, or rather combs her hair, and makes all kinds of gentle noises, murmurings of unspeakable delight. When womanhood dawns, this angel flies away; but sometimes returns, bringing back a little one to mother."

All of these illustrations indicate a special quality beyond our usual interpretation of homemaking. It is homemaking on a celestial plane—and the woman is happy and content.

She also radiates her happiness to others, giving them warmth and contentment. This she does by her presence, singing, smiles, little kindnesses, her bird-like actions as she moves about the house and her gentle words which are of "unspeakable delight." So important does she consider her home life and making it happy that she counts it as "her life's occupation," and is content with this choice. The chief ingredient seems to be that such a woman is happy herself in her homemaking role. This is what a man wants.

Are women in our day happy as homemakers? Generally speaking, they are not. What are their complaints? They say there is no glory in it and little thanks, and that their duties are drudgery and monotonous. They do not feel like goddesses!

Women of high intelligence complain that homemaking requires no talent or special gifts and therefore it offers no challenge. Some feel their calling is outside the home—they turn to the outside world for fulfillment. Men often encourage their dissatisfied wives to work for they want them to be happy.

Why have women failed to find fulfillment in their domestic life? It is because they have not understood its heavenly possibilities. They have thought weeds the rewards, rather than flowers. And they have not understood what man wants in a homemaker. Because of this they fail to please him and this robs them of satisfaction.

Some give the bare stint of requirement—merely feed and clothe the family and sweep and dust. This, of course, requires little intelligence and challenge. It requires gifts of mind and spirit, however, to be a Domestic Goddess, to be the mother of men and create a haven of rest for her husband.

Some unhappy women feel their domestic duties of less importance than men's and therefore they turn their backs on home duties and seek fulfillment in the world's work. Is their attitude a justification for leaving domestic responsibility? Someone has to do woman's work. Someone has to tend their children. Isn't the mother the logical one? She cannot, with any conscience, turn this duty over to someone else.

The role of the Domestic Goddess is a different kind of glory than men enjoy. It is a quiet, unacclaimed honor, but it is the path to rich fulfillment and celestial love.

How to Become a Domestic Goddess

When you take the essential duties of woman and add to them special feminine touches, you produce a Domestic Goddess. What are her essential duties? They are homemaker, mother and wife. The following is the path to their successful fulfillment.

I. *HOMEMAKING*

A. *Duties:*

Housekeeper	Shopper
Cook	Manager of Domestic Money
Seamstress	Laundress

B *How to find happiness in homemaking*: An essential quality of the Domestic Goddess is her ability to find joy and satisfaction in her work. This satisfaction comes as a result of her attitude towards her work and her ability to control her life's activities, as I have expressed in the following thoughts:

1. *Attitude towards drudgery*: Women must face certain tasks which are not joy producers. Every occupation has its boring monotonous tasks and it is best to face them for what they are—a necessary responsibility. It may insult an intelligent woman to indicate she must find her joy in washing diapers and scrubbing floors. Her happiness comes in the overall accomplishment.

Many of our duties, however, are a source of real enjoyment. Caring for children, cooking delicious meals and cleaning the house can all be a happy experience. There are women who delight in scrubbing the floors and walls, washing and ironing and cleaning closets. Actually, little of our work is unpleasant, but when it seems so to you, it is best to face it with an honest attitude, realizing that the world's work consists of a certain amount of drudgery.

2. *Don't become crowded for time*: Some housewives play too many roles outside the home and therefore find it difficult to enjoy homemaking. It may be her own special activities, such as hobbies, clubs or public service organizations which are consuming her time. This is not to say that these things are not

worthwhile when held within limits, but rather to suggest that they can cause her to be crowded for time to enjoy her housework.

Special activities within the home may also crowd her for time to do her more essential duties. Too much time spent talking on the phone, browsing through magazines, watching T.V. or even extensive sewing or canning often cause her to be short on time and in a last-minute rush. When such is the case, it is difficult and often impossible for her to enjoy her work.

Sometimes the wife assumes part of the masculine role, causing her domestic duties to be crowded for time. She may assist her husband in his employment or even take a full time job. Or she may assume some of his home duties, such as yard work, painting, handling his money problems or accounts.

When any of these outside tasks crowd her for time to do her homemaking tasks well, when she hurries through her housework "just to get things done," *it is difficult for her to enjoy her domestic role.*

If you will observe little girls as they play house, you will notice that they do not hurry to get their work finished. They enjoy it too much. They will fold and refold the little blankets, and when they have tucked them neatly around the baby's crib, they will take them all off and start over again. This is because they enjoy what they are doing, and they enjoy it because they are not crowded for time.

If you find yourself saying, "I do not have time to play house as little girls do," then ask yourself, "What am I doing that crowds me for time? Is it more important than my joy in homemaking?"

I do not wish to imply that we live a self-centered life in which we indulge ourselves with pleasures and comforts and our own satisfactions. Giving of ourselves in the service of others is a sacred obligation and brings us great satisfaction in return. There is, nevertheless, much time wasted on foolishness and it is wise to measure each activity for its value, always placing the home duties and their enjoyment as of major importance.

The woman who is happy in her work brings solace and stability to the home. Her children are warmed by her, her husband at peace, and both admire her for the honor she brings to her feminine role.

3. *The Second Mile*: *If you will find joy in your tasks, do them well.* This doctrine was taught hundreds of years ago by Jesus, when He said, "If anyone compel thee to go one mile, go with him twain." Going the second mile lifts the burden out of work and makes it seem easy and enjoyable. *To do well those tasks which are the common lot of all is the truest greatness, and in return brings satisfaction and happiness.*

C *Fundamentals of good homemaking*: The following will result in greater efficiency in homemaking:

1. *Concentration*: The management of an entire household requires concentration. One cannot day dream and ponder problems and at the same time expect duties will be performed with efficiency. There are specific tasks, like ironing in which daydreaming is possible, but most of our work requires thought as well as hands for greatest efficiency.

2. *Organization*: Basic to good homemaking is that of being organized. This would include having a place for everything, a time for everything and some type of a plan or schedule to follow. I know that women dislike rigid schedules, but lack of planning can lead to disorder, hurry and waste of time.

It is doubtful that there is anything about housekeeping so appreciated by the husband than that of a well-organized household, where the home life runs smoothly and without confusion. Some have felt that working diligently and quickly accomplishes such a goal. These virtues are important, but being organized is the secret of a successful homemaker. Time spent in organizing and planning saves hours of time in actual work.

3. *First things first.* Also important is the habit of putting first things first. By this I mean concentrating on the more essential tasks, while placing as secondary those things of lesser importance.

If you will list your six most pressing responsibilities and arrange them in order of their importance, then use it as a guide each day, it will increase efficiency. For example:

1. Appearance
2. Good meals, on time
3. House neat and tidy
4. Washing and ironing
5. Imperative shopping
6. Auxiliary things.

Faithful performance of these duties, in order of their importance will increase efficiency in the home. Other things of lesser importance should not be done at the expense of these greater responsibilities.

There are many things which we allow to interfere with our essential home duties. Such things as talking on the telephone for long periods, sewing to excess, spending hours of time browsing through shops are often the cause of essential home duties being neglected. Some may justify these activities on the grounds that "they enjoy it." Personal sacrifices, however, are often required when one becomes a "Domestic Goddess," but such is the necessary step one takes in becoming Angela Human and earning a man's deepest love.

4. *Simplicity!* Simplicity, Simplicity! You cannot become a good housekeeper if you live in a clutter. I refer to such things as too much furniture, too many dishes, unnecessary clothes, old papers and magazines, too many toys, and endless objects cluttering the house. Or it may be old treasures which are handed down from generation to generation. "Priceless objects," you say. But they are not priceless if they make life difficult. I do not refer to objects of real beauty which enrich our home surroundings. I only refer to those items which offer neither utility nor beauty.

5. *Work:* Although you may concentrate, organize and simplify, you will not accomplish the goal of Domestic Goddess if you are unwilling to work. Good homemaking requires effort, as does any noble achievement. Performing the work, however, is a boon to the woman. *Work is our blessing, not our doom!* It brings spiritual, physical and mental benefits to the individual performing them. For example: A friend who had been having some emotional problems went to a psychiatrist and was given the following advice: "Mrs Jones, I am going to tell you how to relieve your mental disturbances. Go home, take the broom, and clean house." Although this advice cannot be applied in all cases of emotional turmoil, it does prove the value of honest labor. The faithful performance of womanly duties also brings woman inner happiness. It is the upstream swim, or the great efforts of life that lead us to eternal joy. Even the physical body benefits.

D. *The feminine touch*: A man likes a clean well ordered

home, but he also enjoys the feminine touches which are added by the Domestic Goddess.

1. *Cooking*: I have talked to men who have long remembered their mother's cooking—especially for the delicious aroma which they recall. Such things as homemade bread, onions frying, cinnamon rolls baking, arouses sentiment and appreciation. The Italian women are known for their efforts to please their husband's appetites. At times they spend an entire day in the kitchen making a special recipe which is a favorite. And I am told that the Italian women have more gifts showered on them by their men than any other race.

2. *Housekeeping*: Have you ever heard the statement, "You can tell a woman lives here!" Telltale signs like soft pillows, a tempting bowl of fruit, gingham curtains, soft rug before the fireplace, ruffled curtains and artistic pictures and ornaments reveal her feminine touch.

3. *Make him comfortable*: A man's home is his castle! When he comes home he would like the freedom to toss his coat on a chair, sit where he wants to sit, and lie on his own bed without concern for the spread. A woman of my acquaintance was an immaculate housekeeper. Her floors were polished and her house scrubbed, but her husband never felt comfortable in his own home. He divorced her and married a woman who made him feel more comfortable and in comparing the two he had this to say, "The change in women was like taking off a pair of tight shoes and putting on a pair of soft, comfortable slippers."

Allow him the privilege of stacking papers on his desk, or hanging his diplomas on his walls or placing his shoes under the bed if he wishes. If you treat him like the king in his castle, he will treat you like his queen!

II. *MOTHERHOOD*

    A. *Duties*:

Physical care	Personality development
Spiritual training	Fun.

    B. *A grave responsibility*:

"The training of the human soul for advancement and joy here and in the hereafter call for the greatest possible powers of mind and heart. Psychologists and students generally admit that the first years of life are crucial in determining what shall be the future of the child, physically, mentally, and spiritually; that grave responsibility belongs by right of sex to the women who bear and nurture the whole human race. Surely no right thinking woman could crave more responsibility nor greater proof of innate powers than that. . . . Theirs is the right to bear and rear to maturity as well as to influence for good or ill the precious souls of men." (Leah D. Widstoe)

To be a successful mother is greater than to be a successful opera singer, or writer or artist. One is universal and eternal greatness and the other merely phenomenal. Of course, a great mother could become a great artist. But if such secondary greatness is not added to that which is fundamental, it is merely an empty honor.

One day my young son said to me, "Mother, boys are more important than girls, aren't they, for they can become presidents and generals and famous people?" I replied, "But it is mothers who make presidents and statesmen and musicians. The hand that rocks the cradle is the hand that rules the world."

C. *What a man wants:* He wants a wife who delights in bearing him sons and daughters. He may complain and even oppose the birth of more children, but he would like woman to respect her function and not dishonor it. Yet how often does he hear the complaining statement, "Oh, I am so unhappy, I am pregnant again!" Remember, Mumtaz-i-Mahal bore her husband fourteen children.

Not only her willingness to bear children, but her tender care of the children are important to a man. The Domestic Goddess is always conscious and concerned about the physical care of her children, to see that they are properly fed and bathed. She takes pride in the way they look and never allows them to go hungry or cold or neglected.

She is a tender, smiling, gentle, sympathetic mother who teaches her children how to be happy and offers them praise and understanding—giving them bread for their souls as well as their bodies. This is a Domestic Goddess!

D. *How to find joy in your role as mother:* Woman finds fulfillment in her role as mother by going the second mile and doing more than the bare stint of requirements. What is the basic requirement for a child's care? It is to feed and clothe the child. The Domestic Goddess goes far beyond this, giving herself wholeheartedly to patient care and true devotion to the child, and in so doing, finds joy in her role as mother.

III. *WIFE*

A. *Duties*:
> Supporting role to husband
> Loving companion
> Sex partner
> Queen of her household.

The first two of the above duties are covered in the other parts of this book. It is the fourth that is an essential part of woman's role in the home. The term Domestic Goddess implies much more than merely good homemaking and motherhood. It suggests the woman herself as the Queen of her household. There are two qualities which are essential for her in attaining this high position. They are:

B. *Self dignity:* Although the role of woman is one of self sacrifice, there is a quality of self dignity which keeps her role from one of servitude. It is a quality of character which I have referred to as an essential virtue for woman. In connection with the home, it needs particular notice.

There are homes where the woman lacks this self dignity, where she makes a slave of herself for her family, yet who instead of being thanked for it, is rewarded with grudging toleration. She is always called upon to do this or that and is never heard to hesitate. One would think she would be appreciated. Why does her family withhold this honor from her? It is because of her own lack of self respect.

All of us carry an ideal in our minds of what a woman ought to be. But when we see this divine creature, woman, transformed into a mechanical drudge, we cannot help feeling a certain contempt. In her slavery to others, she seems to be paying the natural tribute of an inferior to her superiors, and therefore is not deserving of either thanks or respect.

If, on the other hand, she does not allow others to impose on her and make unfair demands, we look upon her noble sacrifice in the home as one of unselfish character.

C. *Her presence lights the home:* Deruchette had the ability to light up her household. "Her approach was like a cheerful warmth. If woman is to take her place as Queen of her household, she must not appear as a tired, cross, sober and disinterested homemaker."

Do not think that the Domestic Goddess is beyond your capabilities. The Lord assigned you this responsibility, and therefore, has given you every potential for its fulfillment if you will call upon hidden talents and powers.

Our Debt to Society

Although becoming the Domestic Goddess is our prime responsibility, it can become a narrow existence if continued indefinitely with no thought for others. We do owe a certain public good to the world, and it is such benevolence that enriches a woman's life. If the homemaker can increase her efficiency at home so she may help those in need, she will become a better person and even a better mother and wife.

A Matter of Character

It is easy to see that motherhood requires character, but you might not have thought that homemaking does. Good homemaking, however, is essentially a matter of character. For example:

1. *Self-centeredness*: Women who are poor homemakers display lack of character by thinking too much of how they like to spend their time and too little about the feelings and needs of their families. The hours spent talking on the phone, browsing through shops, primping and in other selfish pursuits, while neglecting their home duties indicates a weakness in character.

2. *Lack of organization*: God is our pattern of perfection. He demonstrates the importance of orderliness in all of his creations, from the human body to the planets in the heavens. He says, "I am a God of order, not confusion." Failure to follow this eternal example indicates lack of character.

3. *Lack of knowledge*: A lack of knowledge does not justify the poor housekeeper. Her unwillingness to learn, to seek, to knock and search for the knowledge that she lacks shows further weakness of character.

The role of the Domestic Goddess is a spiritual qualification, as is indicated in the following Biblical quotation:

Who can find a virtuous woman?
>for her price is far above rubies.
The heart of her husband doth safely
>trust in her
So that he shall have no need of spoil.

She seeketh wool and flax
>and worketh willingly with her hands
She is like the merchant ships
>she bringeth her food from afar
She riseth also while it is yet night
>and giveth meat to her household.

Her candle goeth not out by night
She layeth her hands to the spindle
>and her hands hold the distaff
She stretcheth out her hand to the poor
>yea, she reacheth forth her hands to the needy,
She is not afraid of the snow
>for her household
For all her household are clothed
>with scarlet.
She maketh herself coverings
>of tapestry;
Her clothing is silk and purple.

She looketh well to the ways of her
>household
And eateth not the bread of idleness
Her children rise up and call her
>blessed.
Her husband also, and he
>praiseth her.
Many daughters have done virtuously
>but thou excelleth them all.

>(Proverbs 31)

Rewards

Although becoming a domestic goddess may require effort, it is not a sacrifice, for as in other phases of Fascinating Womanhood, rich rewards follow. Especially in the fulfillment of the womanly role is the woman blessed, for therein lies her real happiness. The following expressions will illustrate:

SUCCESS STORY

I now know what I am doing on this earth and what happiness can come to a woman. Before, I never felt a woman was anything but a "Yes, dear" dummy. I couldn't be happy this way and it resulted in my being in competition with men and especially with my husband. I made the decisions for us and tried to help my husband, and made every effort to convince him that I had a brain on my shoulders. All of this sent me further from what I really wanted—his love.

How much easier it is now. How much more fun it is to have my whole day to do for him the things I should. I hated to lose the romantic days of our engagement and early marriage, but its coming back, just as you said it would. I now enjoy being a woman. Its really fun.

SUCCESS STORY

I believe most women have a crisis in their life, or reach a point when they come face to face with the realization that they do not feel fulfilled. I would guess this is why so many women leave home for the glamour of the working world. I had no such desires but did feel rather like a drudge. I was seeking for the true purpose of woman. Was it just to bear children and do the never ending housework? I felt somewhat indispensible and yet I couldn't convince myself that this inferior role was my lot in life. Fascinating Womanhood has taught me the heavenly possibilities which are in store for women. I have been so thrilled with the results.

SUCCESS STORY

In the past, I have felt that motherhood was about the only real joy of womanhood for me. I used to envy men and their role in life and society. I felt trapped at home and resentful that women were placed in obedience to men. This new concept and respect for my sex is one of the most wonderful things that has happened to me. Already my marriage is happier than I could have believed possible. My husband has a new spring in his step and a new note of authority in his voice which is thrilling to behold, and I am finally really satisfied and happy with being a woman.

Assignment

List in order of importance your six most essential responsibilities. If you are not certain how they should be placed, consult your husband for his interpretation.

Part II

THE HUMAN QUALITIES

1. *Femininity*

2. *Radiates happiness*

3. *Fresh appearance and manner*

4. *Childlikeness*

The Human side of woman fascinates, amuses, captivates and enchants man. It arouses a desire to protect and shelter.

A man wants an angel but he also wants a woman who is human. He is human himself, and therefore, certain of these qualities appeal to him and arouse his fascination.

The Human side is *what a woman does,* and includes her appearance, her manner and her actions. It is her extreme girlishness, her dependency upon man, her delicacy and her femininity. It is also her joyfulness, vivacity and her teasing playfulness. Add to all this a rosy glow of vibrant health and a dash of spunk and sauciness and an underlying attitude of trust and tenderness and you begin to build a delightfully human creature—one that will win man's heart.

The human qualities fascinate men. They enchant him, captivate him, and amuse him, and also arouse in him a tender feeling—a desire to protect and shelter. They set off a spark, or a driving force in man, and at times cause him to do what appears to be foolish things. It is now that love is blind. This is the mad infatuation and indulgence that can lead him to a pinnacle of joy, or destruction.

The Human qualities, in some instances, will cause a man of intelligence and character to marry a girl of inferior qualities—perhaps some brainless doll whom he finds irresistable. One would expect such a man to choose a more sensible companion, but her Human appeal has made love blind. The fascination David Copperfield had for Dora was due to her Human characteristics, and caused him to turn from the angelic Agnes to marry Dora.

The Human qualities have tremendous appeal. If anything can be said for them, it is that they have more power over the average man than the Angelic.

These are not difficult to acquire; they are not foreign to your nature, for they are woman's natural instincts. If you do not have them, it is because they have been suppressed.

They are not "unholy," for they enrich man's life, and when combined with the Angelic cause a man to experience *celestial love.*

CHAPTER XIV

Femininity

THE GENTLE, TENDER QUALITY

Femininity is a gentle, tender quality found in a woman's appearance, manner and actions and her general attitude. No other quality has so much appeal to men, for it is such a direct contrast to his own strong and firm masculinity. This contrast, when brought to his attention causes him to feel manly, and this realization of his own masculinity is one of the most enjoyable sensations he can experience. The extremely feminine woman is charming to men, and the woman who is completely lacking in it may even be repulsive to men.

Femininity is acquired by *accentuating the differences between yourself and men, not the similarities.* You apply this principle in your appearance, your manner, your actions and even your attitude. The more different you appear than men the more feminine you become.

1. THE FEMININE APPEARANCE

To be most fascinating to men, women must wear only those materials and styles which are the least suggestive of those used by the men and which therefore make the greatest contrast to men's apparel.

1. *Materials:*

a. *Weave:* Those to avoid are tweeds, herringbones, hard finish woolens, and denims. Materials which are the extremes of femininity are chiffon, silk, lace, velvet, satin, fur, angora, and organdie. These can be worn when trying to make the most feminine appeal, but are certainly not appropriate for every occasion. Cottons, soft woolens and synthetics can be feminine according to their weave.

b. *Colors:* Colors which are strictly feminine are pastels and vivid colors. Others can be worn if weave, design or basic style are feminine.

c. *Design:* Floral prints and polk-a-dots are strictly feminine. Others vary. Those to avoid are glen plaids, faint dark plaids, pin stripes, shepherd checks, herringbones and certain geometrics. However, they can be used if basic style or color is feminine.

2. *Style:*

a. *Basic style:* Avoid tailored styles or any suggestion of masculinity such as buttoned cuffs, lapels and top stitching. These styles can be used, however, if an extreme feminine color or fabric such as velvet or lace is used. The effect can be quite charming. Extreme feminine styles are such things as full skirts, ruffles, scallops, puffed sleeves, gathers, drapes, flowing trains and many others. These styles are not always in fashion, nor are they practical for all occasions. There are, however, feminine styles always available which we may use for any occasion. The dress itself is feminine, since men do not wear them.

It is difficult to advise a feminine style which would be suitable for all women, since we vary in figure. A safe standard would be to avoid a resemblance to masculinity, and when a most feminine style is desired, choose one quite opposite to masculinity.

I noticed a lady in the grocery store one morning in what I considered a most feminine style. Her dress was of black linen, simply cut, and around the v-neck was a white, chiffon collar, double layered and quite full. She appeared to me soft, lovely and entirely appropriate for her morning shopping.

Should women wear pants? They are not feminine in style. If they are worn, however, they should be of feminine color or fabric and worn with a blouse or top which softens the masculine effect.

b. *Trim:* Trim can give a feminine effect to an otherwise plain dress. Lace, ribbons, colorful ties, fringe, embroidery, beads, and many types of braid express a feminine look.

3. *Accessories:* Avoid purses which resemble men's brief cases and shoes of masculine style. Wear soft scarfs, flowers, jewelry, ribbons.

The important thing to consider is the over-all *impression* which you give. Work for softness, airiness, delicacy and striking contrast to masculinity. The effect can be fascinating to a man.

A mother told me that when her young son viewed an extreme of femininity he said to his mother, with awakened emotion, "Oh, Mother, look! She looks so soft!"

The Femininity of the Little Girl

The appeal which a little girl of four makes in a plain, soiled dress, ragged stockings, untidy hair is quite different from the appeal which the same child makes on Sunday, when dressed in lovely pink bonnet, soft organdie dress, with little pink knees dimpling above little socks and shiny slippers, and with dainty ribbon and freshly curled hair setting off her bright little face. You might look upon the every-day child with indifference, but you cannot resist the impulse to gather up the Sunday child and press her to your heart. Now, if this same Sunday child instead of dressing in the lovely Sunday outfit described, should be arrayed in sleek tailored black dress, a severely plain dark hat, with her hair plastered down close to her head, she would hardly make any appeal whatever.

What you should have is apparel that will never let him forget that you are a woman. You should emphasize this fact as much as possible throughout the day. This principle should be applied to every item of your dress, from shoes to comb to apron to house dress and elaborate social dress.

Men are effected by modern trends and may prefer that you dress conservatively in public, but usually they have secret desires or whims of how they would like you to dress at home or on special occasions. My grandfather wanted my grandmother to have a red velvet dress but she was too conservative to heed his wish.

2. The Feminine Manner

I have pointed out the fundamentals of feminine dress and appearance, but if you do not add to this the feminine manner, the total effect can be irritating or even humorous. We have all seen women who wear the most feminine dresses, but who wear them as if they were on the wrong person. They do not carry themselves generally in a way to harmonize with their clothes. They are *"professors in chiffon, bears in lace, or wooden posts in organdie."*

What is the feminine manner? It is the motions of a

woman's body, the way she uses her hands, her walk, her talk, the sound of her voice, her facial expressions, her laugh. It seems to be more important than that of appearance, for it is a greater contrast to masculine strength and firmness.

David Copperfield was fascinated by Dora's enchanting manner. The way she patted the horses, spanked her little dog, or held her flowers against her chin were attractive to him. "She had the most delightful little voice, the gayest little laugh, the pleasantest and most fascinating little ways."

A GLIMPSE INTO FEMININITY

In the *Cloister and the Hearth,* by Charles Reade, is an illustration of the thrilling sensation the feminine manner can awaken in man.

"Then came a little difficulty; Gerard could not tie his ribbon again as Catherine [his mother] had tied it. Margaret, after slyly eyeing his efforts for some time, offered to help him; for at her age girls love to be coy and tender, saucy and gentle by turns, . . . then a fair head, with its stately crown of auburn curls, glossy and glowing through silver, bowed sweetly towards him; and while it ravished his eye, two white supple hands played delicately upon the stubborn ribbon, and moulded it with soft and airy touches. *Then a heavenly thrill ran through the innocent young man, and vague glimpses of a new world of feeling and sentiment opened to him.* — And these new exquisite sensations Margaret unwittingly prolonged; it is not natural to her sex to hurry ought that pertains to the sacred toilet. Nay, when the taper fingers had at last subjugated the ends of the knot, her mind was not quite easy till, by a maneuver peculiar to the female hand, she had made her palm convex and so applied it with a gentle pressure to the center of the knot—a sweet little coaxing hand kiss, as much as to say, 'Now be a good knot, and stay so! . . . There, that was how it was!' said Margaret, and drew back to take one last survey of her work; then looking up for simple approval of her skill, received full in her eyes a *longing gaze of such adoration* as made her lower them quickly and color all over."

HOW TO ACQUIRE A FEMININE MANNER

You acquire a feminine manner by accentuating the differences between yourself and men, not the similarities. Since men are strong, tough, firm and heavy in manner, you must be delicate, tender, gentle, and light. You show this by the way you walk, talk, use your hands and carry yourself generally.

1. *The hands*: We have seen how Dora and Margaret charmed men with the use of their hands. We use our hands so constantly that it is of course an important part of the feminine manner. The manner in which you shake hands with men is important. There should be gentleness and never firmness and strength. Although you are trying to fascinate only your own husband, you will have to make femininity a consistent part of your personality. He will be proud of the feminine impression which you give to others, for it will command their respect. And when you take a man's arm, place yours lightly on his and do not use him as a support, as you would a crutch.

2. *The walk*: The most important part of the feminine manner is the walk. Deruchette had the "graceful repose of the West Indian woman." Imagine that you weigh 95 pounds! The many points stressed in charm classes, such as toes pointing forward, walk a straight line with head erect—add to charm, but they are not as essential to femininity as is lightness, softness and grace.

3. *The voice*: Dora had "a delightful little voice." The feminine voice is gentle, tender and variable. It can be high and bubbling, or soft and mellow and at times even whispery, but it is never firm, loud or harsh.

4. *The laugh:* There are some women who laugh in a very unfeminine manner. They open their mouths wide, throw back their heads, close their eyes and roar. If these extremes are avoided the laugh will probably be at least acceptable.

5. *The cooing or purring quality:* This is an extreme feminine quality which is reserved for only your man. Deruchette "made all kinds of gentle noises, murmurings of unspeakable delight to certain ears." It is an intimate type of conversation and is soothing and feminine to man. It is a kittenish or purring quality of a woman's voice.

6. *Facial expressions*: Harshness, bitterness, fierce frowns and tightness across the lips all reveal an unwholesome character and *destroy feminine charm.* On the other hand, tender eyes, a

gentle smile, and serene expression all reveal the gentle tender quality of the spirit and therefore are feminine.

7. *Conversation*: Your conversation and your facial expressions are the human expressions of a gentle, tender spirit. It must radiate from the soul, but it does so through the feminine manner. It is the crowning glory of the feminine woman and is important with husband, children and everyone she meets.

FEMININE CONVERSATION WITH CHILDREN

The gentle, tender, patient mother is the feminine one. Do not wait for some extreme emergency to show such tenderness for your children. When your little boy passes by, pat him on the head and say, "You little dear," or take your little girl in your arms and say, "You are just the kind of little girl I always wanted." Or rest your hands on your older son's shoulders and say, "What a fine boy you are, I am so proud of you." These things should not be said occasionally, but daily! Be kind, sympathetic and understanding with them in their special problems, and deliberately see that they have a steady diet of tenderness from you. This will help keep your children from going astray, and will develop your feminine side more than anything you can do. Bossiness, crossness and harshness do not make for good behavior and they *destroy feminine charm*.

THE FEMININE APPROACH WITH YOUR HUSBAND

The tender, feminine approach of a woman can tame the most difficult man. The following story will illustrate:

THE TIGER'S WHISKER—
AN OLD KOREAN TALE

"The story is of Yun Ok, a married girl who came to the house of a wise sage for council. Her problem was this:

" 'It is my husband, wise one,' she said. 'He is very dear to me. For the past three years he has been away fighting in the wars. Now that he has returned he hardly speaks to me, or to anyone else. If I speak, he doesn't seem to hear. When he talks at all, it is roughly. If I serve him food not to his liking, he pushes it aside, and angrily leaves the room. Sometimes when he should be working in the rice field, I see him sitting idly on top of the hill, looking towards the sea! I want a potion,' she said, 'so he will be loving and gentle as he used to be.'

"The wise sage instructed the young woman to get for him the whisker of a living tiger, from which he would make the magic potion.

"At night, when her husband was asleep, she crept from her house with a bowl of rice and meat sauce in her hand. She went to the place on the mountainside where the tiger was known to live. Standing far off from the tiger's cave, she held out the bowl of food, calling the tiger to come and eat, but the Tiger did not come.

"Each night she returned, doing the same thing and each time a few steps closer. Although the tiger did not come to eat, he did become accustomed to seeing her there.

"One night she approached within a stone's throw of the cave. This time the tiger came a few steps toward her and stopped. The two of them stood looking at one another in the moonlight. It happened again the following night and this time they were so close that she could talk to him in a soft, soothing voice.

"The next night, after looking carefully into her eyes, the tiger ate the food that she held out for him. After that, when Yun Ok came in the night she found the tiger waiting for her on the trail. Nearly six months had passed since the night of her first visit. At last, one night after caressing the animal's head, she said, 'Oh, generous animal, I must have one of your whiskers. Do not be angry with me.' And she snipped off one of the whiskers.

"The tiger did not become angry as she had feared that he might. She went down the trail, running with the whisker tightly clutched in her hand. When she brought it to the wise sage, he examined it to see if it was real, then tossed it into the fire, causing the poor girl to become stunned. Then the sage said, 'Yun Ok, is a man more vicious than a tiger? Is he less responsive to kindness and understanding? If you can win the love and confidence of a wild and bloodthirsty animal by gentleness and patience, surely you can do the same with your husband.' "

It is surprising to see how few women realize the potential of their femininity. We often see men and women engaged in vicious combat as though they were bloodthirsty animals. But with such a powerful weapon as femininity, a woman is rather short sighted to use claws and fangs.

BEWITCHING LANGUOR

Languor is a feminine characteristic and is a relaxed, calm, quiet air, similar to that of a cat relaxing before a fireplace. It is like a touch of velvet and is calming and appealing to men. "Deruchette had at times an air of bewitching languor." Languor is a means of varying other feminine mannerisms.

The opposite of languor is the nervous, high-strung woman who is always biting fingernails, jingling her keys, twisting her handkerchief or twisting her hair.

DON'TS AND DO'S FOR THE FEMININE MANNER

don't	*do*
1. Slap men on the back	1. Shake hands with men gracefully
2. Whistle loudly	2. Speak softly, tenderly
3. Roar at jokes	3. Walk lightly
4. Yell	4. Eat quietly
5. Gulp food	5. Take a man's arm lightly
6. Drink by throwing your head back	6. Look tenderly
7. Lean heavily on a man's arm	7. Make tender statements to your children
8. Grasp a man's hand tightly	8. When your husband is harsh, respond with the power of femininity.
9. Walk heavily	
10. Look fierce or hard	
11. Speak harshly	

ASSIGNMENT

If your husband is harsh, say, tenderly, "You poor dear, I think you must have had a hard day."

Say to your children:

Girl, any age,   "How's my sweet, little girl today?"

Boy, young   "You're a dear boy. Did you know that I am very proud of you?"

Boy, older   "It's wonderful to have a strong, capable son like you!"

CHAPTER XV

Feminine Dependency

Feminine dependency is the feminine actions of a woman. It can best be described by saying, "It is her lack of masculine ability." The role of man, we have learned, is to lead, protect and provide for woman. Her need for his manly care is called feminine dependency.

Do not think that protecting a dependent woman is an imposition on a man. *The most pleasant sensation a real man can experience is his consciousness of the power to give his manly care and protection. Rob him of this sensation of superior strength and ability and you rob him of his manliness.* It is a delight to him to protect and shelter a dependent woman. The bigger, manlier and more sensible a man is, the more he seems to be attracted by this quality.

How Men Feel in the Presence of Capable Women

What happens when the average red-blooded man comes in contact with an obviously able, intellectual and competent woman manifestly independent of any help a mere man can give and capable of meeting him or defeating him upon his own ground? He simply doesn't feel like a man any longer. In the presence of such strength and ability in a mere woman, he feels like a futile, ineffectual imitation of a man. It is the most uncomfortable and humiliating sensation a man can experience; so that the woman who arouses it becomes repugnant to him.

A man cannot derive any joy or satisfaction from protecting a woman who can obviously do very well without him. He only delights in protecting or sheltering a woman who needs his manly care, or at least appears to need it.

How Men Feel in the Presence of Dependent Women

When a man is in the presence of a tender, gentle, trustful, dependent woman, he immediately feels a sublime expansion of his power to protect and shelter this frail and delicate creature. In the presence of such weakness he feels stronger, more competent, bigger, manlier than ever. This feeling of strength and power is the most enjoyable he can experience. The apparent need of the woman for protection, instead of arousing contempt for her lack of ability, appeals to the very noblest feelings within him.

AMELIA

A perfect illustration of feminine dependency in woman is in the character of Amelia in *Vanity Fair*. The following is a description of her and the charm she possessed in men's eyes.

"Those who formed the small circle of Amelia's acquaintances were quite angry with the enthusiasm with which the other sex regarded her. For almost all men who came near her loved her; though no doubt they would be at a loss to tell you why. She was not brilliant, nor witty, nor wise overmuch, nor extraordinarily handsome. But wherever she went she touched and charmed everyone of the male sex, as invariably as she awakened the scorn and incredulity of her own sisterhood. I think it was her *weakness* which was her principle charm; a kind of *sweet submission* and *softness* which seemed to appeal to each man she met for his sympathy and protection."

MRS. WOODROW WILSON

Mrs. Wilson was a tender, dependent woman, for her husband wrote to her, "What a source of steadying and of strength it is to me in such seasons of too intimate self-questioning to have one fixed point of confidence and certainty—that even, unbroken, excellent perfection of my little wife, with her poise, her easy capacity in action, her unfailing courage, her quick efficient thought—and the charm that goes with it all, the sweetness, the feminine grace,—none of the usual penalties of efficiency—no hardness, no incisive sharpness, no air of command or of unyielding opinion. Most women who are efficient are such terrors."

THE EFFICIENT WOMAN THAT MEN ADMIRE

Occasionally, we may notice men who seem to admire women who are efficient and capable. Don't let this confuse you.

Although the man may have a genuine admiration for such a woman, it does not mean he finds her attractive. He undoubtedly admires her as he would another man—with appreciation for her fine ability.

How Do We Acquire Feminine Dependency?

1. *Manner and attitude:* You must dispense with any air of strength and ability, of competence and fearlessness and acquire instead an air of frail dependency upon man to take care of you. The air of being able to "kill their own snakes" is just what destroys the charm of so many professional women. And it is the absence of this air that permits many a senseless doll to capture an able and intelligent man whom one would expect to choose a more sensible companion.

Women often display a capable attitude in the things they say. For example, there are women who oppose life insurance, with the excuse, "Oh, if anything happened to you, I could take care of myself well enough." Or in planning a trip, or a move, they take no thought of needing masculine care or protection.

2. *Prove your dependency by the following methods:*

   a. Stop doing masculing tasks and duties.

   b. When "stuck" with a masculine job, do it in a "feminine manner."

a. Eliminating the Man's Work

To attain the quality of feminine dependency it is essential that you eliminate masculine work. If you have assumed such responsibility for years it may seem difficult to make a complete change, but do eliminate as many jobs as possible and especially the more strenuous tasks. I refer to such things as mowing the lawn, painting, carrying heavy boxes, carpentry, earning a portion of the living, making major decisions, handling the money problems and worries, making a long distance trip alone, braving the dark, facing the creditors, and repairing the furnace.

It is important that you cease these more strenuous masculine tasks. "Oh," you might say, "I've tried that, but it doesn't work. Why, I stopped mowing the lawn and the grass grew a foot high. And if I didn't paint my own kitchen, it would never get painted. He won't do these things for me so I have to resort to doing them myself." This is the common response.

The trouble lies in the fact that the woman does not stop completely, but only temporarily. She never *lets go* and turns her back to man's responsibilities. "But," you again might say, "If I do not do them and he does not, what will happen? Someone must do these things."

But must they? Must the lawn be mowed and the kitchen painted and the battles won at the expense of feminine charm? Woman must learn to turn her back completely to these tasks unless through widowhood it becomes a pressing emergency.

Nor should you become critical of your husband if he fails to perform his masculine duties. They are his to do or neglect as he wishes. If this failure on his part is difficult for you to accept, eliminate your critical attitude by saying to yourself, "Have I performed my tasks well today? Was I dressed and well groomed before breakfast? Did I serve my husband well pre-pared meals on time today? Is my house clean and orderly? Have I been patient with my children? Am I loving and under-standing of my husband?" After you have answered these ques-tions then ask, "Do I have the right to feel resentful because he neglects his duties?"

"But," you might say again, "I cannot stand for the roof to leak and the door to fall from its hinges and the lawn to go unmowed." If you cannot make these temporary sacrifices, you cannot become Angela Human—nor can you awaken a man's chivalry. All of these material objects will one day be dust, but your marriage, if you lay the necessary groundwork, may last throughout eternity.

In making the first step to "let go" of masculine responsibil-ity, it is best and only fair to go to your husband and express yourself. Tell him that you feel "unfeminine" doing these things and that you want very much to become a truly feminine woman and live within the bounds of your own role. Then ask him, in a very sweet manner, if he will do these things for you.

This request is very appealing to a man and will undoubt-edly cause him to express cooperation. How much better this is than to complain and make him feel ashamed for neglecting his manly duties, or to pressure him to get them done.

After making the request, don't expect any miracles, and don't keep hammering the point. If he neglects his duties, face it with the attitude I have described above.

b. Masculine Tasks Performed "In a Feminine Manner"

In returning to a quality of dependency there may be times that you will feel "stuck" with some masculine job. If you must do it, then prove your dependency by doing it in a "feminine manner." By this, I mean, do it as a *real feminine woman* would. It isn't up to you to perform these masculine tasks with the skill that men do. If you must paint, repair the furnace, fix the car, the roof, or handle the family finances, do not try so hard to do it with masculine efficiency. Just be yourself—your true feminine self, and your husband will soon realize that you need masculine assistance. Women are supposed to be inferior in the masculine duties. If you are not, it is because you have taken on unnatural capability. I will illustrate how this can be done by the following examples:

CUP HOLDER

A girl who had been doing the manly chores took her first step towards proving her dependency by the following: She attached a paper cup dispenser on the wall upside down. When her husband came home he said, "Say, this isn't on right! Why did you mount it upside down?" Then she said, "Oh, how do you tell which is right side up?" He immediately took out the screw driver and mounted it right.

THE PLANTER BOX

Another woman built a wooden planter box but she failed to saw the boards straight. When her husband saw it, he was amused. Was he ashamed of her inferior work? No! He was delighted, for it made him feel superior.

SUCCESS STORY

A working wife was fired from her job. She said, "Oh, I just can't go out in the world again and get another—they might fire me again. What will I do?" Her husband felt an expansion of his ability, went to his employer and said, "My wife has been fired and I am going to have to look for work that will be sufficient to support my wife and children." The employer asked, "What was your wife's salary?" The man told him the amount, and the employer increased his salary to cover the difference. Just one of the many solutions to problems when you make a man feel like one.

SUMMARY

I have told you that man wants a dependent, feminine wife, for such a woman causes him to feel an enjoyable sense of manliness. I have also told you that man is uncomfortable in the presence of capable women—for they make him feel like an imitation of a man. I have explained that you acquire this quality of dependency by your attitude and that you prove your dependency by ceasing the masculine tasks and retaining the lesser ones for further proof. If you want to become the truly feminine woman—if you want to become Angela Human, you will have to eventually eliminate all masculine tasks except where there is a compelling emergency.

REWARDS

1. It will make your husband feel manly.
2. It will arouse a sense of chivalry—he will offer his protection.
3. You will acquire a portion of the charm of Angela Human which will bring you one step closer to his Celestial love.

When a man protects a feminine woman, he naturally loves her more. This is true of any individual that protects or shelters any form of life that is in need of protection. Take our pets for example. Don't we learn to love them by taking care of them? And the more helplessly dependent they are on us the more tenderly we feel for them. Take a little canary for example. Don't you love him because he is so trustingly dependent upon you for food and water, because his happiness is so obvious when he is rewarded with a bit of food, because he is so flutteringly timid, and because he twists his little head with such an air of interest and alertness, and because with all his self importance he is so helplessly dependent upon you that you cannot think of trusting his care to anyone else. This feeling magnified a thousand times is what everyone feels that protects and shelters another, whether it is the child that protects a pet or the mother who protects her children or the husband who protects his wife.

SHOULD WOMEN BE TRAINED FOR WORK?

Since women charm men by being dependent, the question will arise should they be trained to work?

Many parents feel that they should prepare their daughters to make a living in the event of widowhood, divorce or other compelling emergencies. But consider the seriousness of this step from the following viewpoints:

1. If she is independent she is less inclined to go through the adjustments that many marriages must make. Working may appear an easy way out.

2. It does not appear logical that woman should bypass the cultural education, the classes which would make her a better wife, mother and citizen and train for a rare emergency. Man might as well train for motherhood and homemaking if this logic is sound.

3. The woman who has the cultural education is more apt to increase her creativeness, her intelligence and wisdom. This special ability helps her find her way into the working world when the need arises. She has more ingenuity in an emergency.

4. Requirements for employment change from year to year. The woman who is qualified at one time—may be "out of date" a few years later, and must return for further training to qualify herself for work.

5. Training for careers encourages women to work. The effort she has put forth in training seems wasted if it is "put on the shelf."

With these facts in view, it seems logical that woman should be trained as wife, mother, homemaker as well as good citizen, rather than for a specific career. This training will not detract from her feminine charm, but will enrich it.

THE SWEET PROMISE

Although a man wants a dependent wife, he also would like the knowledge that if left a widow she would have enough strength of character to "carry on" and not become bewildered with her situation.

This knowledge is called the "sweet promise." It is an assurance of her Angelic side which helps to balance the dependency of her Human side. It is a conviction that she could, if necessary, be very brave and face desperate emergencies with womanly courage. Although she is delicate, she would never let her little ones want for the necessities, and would protect them with her very life if necessary.

AN ILLUSTRATION

Take for example a young widow who is left with several small children to support. What does she do? She sets out single handed to battle against all odds. She slaves and struggles, she dares and she suffers in her efforts to provide for her children. When defeat stares her in the face she doesn't even whimper, but taking her lot as a matter of course, grimly clenches her teeth and braves the struggle again. No matter what pain she suffers from overwork she has always a smile of comfort for the childish fears of her little ones; no matter how weary she is, she is always ready to forget her own weariness at the slightest hint of danger to one of her children.

This Sweet Promise is a quality which should shine through a woman's character in a way that man can detect it. It comes from the development of the Angelic qualities.

ASSIGNMENT

1. Eliminate masculine tasks and duties.
2. If "stuck" with a masculine job, prove your feminine dependency by doing it in a feminine manner.
3. Say: "I am certainly happy that I have a man to do the things *which I cannot do*." If you need a heavy object lifted, say, "Will you please loan me your muscular strength for I don't believe that I can lift this."

Remember that by nature you are not capable. If you have any masculine capabilities, you have acquired them un-naturally. God did not create woman for the strenuous masculine responsibilities.

The quality of dependency is the counterpart of man's feeling of superiority. These two feelings then are tied together. In other words, you make man feel superior in his role as man by becoming dependent.

Radiant Happiness

I have already told you of deep inner happiness which is a spiritual quality and must be earned. What then is radiant happiness?

Radiant happiness is a human quality and is therefore voluntary. It is cheerfulness, laughter, singing, joyfulness, smiles, bright eyes, pleasant outlooks, hope, optimism and the ability to radiate joy to others. . . .

DERUCHETTE, AMELIA AND DORA

Deruchette "shed joy around and cast light upon dark days; her presence lights the home; her approach is like a cheerful warmth; she passes by and we are content; she stays awhile and we are happy." Amelia was "kind, fresh and smiling, with a smiling heart." Dora had a "gay little laugh and a delightful little voice."

Mrs. Woodrow Wilson also had this quality, for her husband said, "She was so radiant, so happy!"

Men do not like to see women sober, too serious and gloomy. They want a woman who is *vibrant, alive and happy*. This is an essential part of the real charm that men find fascinating in women.

Many of us are happy at heart but it has never occurred to us that it is important to radiate it to others. We put our happiness "under a bushel" rather than "on a candlestick." Since radiant happiness is voluntary, it can be acquired by habit.

HOW TO ACQUIRE RADIANT HAPPINESS

1. *Work for inner happiness:* It is difficult to radiate happiness to others if you are unhappy at heart. You can smile, but the other traits of radiance will seem unnatural if you are basically unhappy. You attain inner happiness by the development of

the character. Therefore, this is the necessary groundwork—at least to a degree—for acquiring radiant happiness.

2. *The smile.* Deruchette and Amelia were not beautiful girls, but both had smiles which were an outstanding mark of their loveliness. Deruchette had a "smile which none know how, had the power to lighten the weight of that enormous chain which all the living in common drag behind them, a dangerous smile which was Deruchette herself." Amelia was "a smiling goddess, with a smiling heart. Her lips had the freshest of smiles."

3. *The eyes.* Along with Amelia's smile, Thackeray says her "eyes sparkled with the brightest and honestest of good humor." The smile, therefore, was not only of the lips, but of the entire countenance.

Other means of radiating happiness are your cheerful words, your expressions, your optimistic attitudes and outlooks and your song. The woman who sings to her household brings the cheerful message that "all is well" in her heart.

THE REAL CHARM

Inner happiness combined with radiant happiness is an essential part of the real charm that men find fascinating in women. Inner happiness as we have learned brings a calm spirit and tranquility which is a peaceful beauty. It is like clear calm water in a pond. But radiant happiness is like the lily pads that add breathtaking beauty. Beneath the flowers you can see the stillness of the waters. But the charm is in the overall effect.

There is in this world no function more important than that of being charming—to shed joy around, to cast light upon dark days, to be the golden thread of our destiny, and the very spirit of grace and harmony. Is not this to render a service?

CHAPTER XVII

Fresh Radiant Health

A fresh appearance is essential to womanly beauty. The woman who appears wilted or drab is not attractive to men. There must be in the entire appearance and manner of woman a fresh, clean over-all effect.

Amelia radiated this healthy beauty, for her "smile was fresh, her voice was fresh, her eyes sparkled and her face blushed with rosy health." Deruchette was "fresh and joyous as the lark."

GOOD HEALTH

The foundation of fresh beauty is genuine good health. Not only for the health itself, but for the fresh and joyous spirit health sustains in the woman's appearance, actions and attitude. How alluring are sparkling and dancing eyes, lustrous hair, clear voice, buoyancy of manner and the animation which good health brings to the face and the vivacity it communicates to the thoughts. We cannot, therefore, attach too much importance to this qualification.

We all know the importance of good health, but our trouble lies in thinking of good health in terms of not being ill. But the perfection of healthy womanhood is more than merely being well. A fresh radiant appearance is a result of health in rich abundance.

Health, like happiness, is based upon laws, and comes as a result of understanding and applying them. The following are the fundamentals:

Fundamentals of Good Health

1. Correct internal disorders
2. Get enough sleep
3. Exercise
4. Drink plenty of water

5. Fresh air
6. Eat properly
7. Relax—at work or play
8. Have a healthy mental attitude

1. *Correct internal disorders:* It is impossible to attain health if there are internal disorders. Often women will go for years with such things as infected teeth or internal organs, disorders of the blood or the glands and other malfunctions of the body which causes them to have poor health. Many of these ailments can be eliminated by proper attention.

2. *Get enough sleep:* We all know the value of sufficient sleep but married women often neglect this essential, putting other things first in importance. If you are robbed of your sleep by too many things to do, ask yourself if your tasks are more important than you are. Is the dress more important than the dressmaker? Is the house more important than the housekeeper? Although a man appreciates a clean home, he does not want it at the expense of feminine charm. Many of our activities are a waste of time when measured against genuine good health.

3. *Exercise:* You may feel that you have enough exercise in the varied activities of housework such as bending, reaching and walking. But these motions do not bring all the muscles into play. As a result, married women suffer poor posture, sagging muscles, fat deposits and loss of health. If exercise seems like merely an added labor to your already busy day, remember that exercise can actually rest a weary person. Calling a different set of muscles into activity refreshes and stimulates the body.

4. *Drink plenty of water:* The body is made up of 66 percent water—more than two thirds by weight, and several gallons in all. If you do not drink enough water your body will be forced to use its water over and over again. Your whole system will suffer unless refreshed frequently with a new supply of water. If you will measure three quarts of water each morning and consume the entire amount during the day, you can be certain of having enough water.

5. *Fresh air:*

   a. *Air supply:* Proper air supply includes both oxygen and moisture. Most of us realize the importance of fresh air both night and day, but many do not realize how essential is its moisture content. Many modern heating systems dry the air which can result in irritations to the respiratory system, causing colds, sore throats and even lung irritation. There are several solutions: (1) turn the furnace off at night and open the windows; (2) have a moisturizer installed in the furnace; and (3) use a vaporizer or hang wet towels in the bedrooms at night. The same care need be taken if the furnace is used in the daytime.

    b. *Breathe deeply:* Although you may have a good air supply, your lungs may fail to be replenished unless you breathe deeply. Poor posture and lack of exercise can cause this shallow breathing and it is therefore important to make some conscious effort to see that your lungs get enough air. Oxygen is our most important food. What good food is to the stomach, oxygen is to the blood. The body that is starved for oxygen cannot possibly be healthy.

6. *Eat properly:* What is a safe guide for proper eating? Our appetite is not a safe guide, for even bad foods taste good. There are many foods and products on the market. Which are good and which ones harmful? Many of the studies concerning foods are confusing and some of them are contradictory.

Nature reveals to us the secrets of good eating. We cannot improve on an apple as it comes from a tree or a banana or a potato as it comes from the earth. *Eat foods as near to nature as possible* is the safest rule. There is fresh food available in every season. The summer brings its fruits, vegetables and melons; the fall brings apples, squash and potatoes which last until spring. Early spring brings the navel oranges, late spring the berries and more fresh vegetables. All of these are best when eaten fresh in the season in which they grow. Nature also produces the grains which remain fresh for several seasons.

Wholesome foods fall into five categories:
        fresh fruits
        fresh vegetables
        nuts
        grains
        meats

There are many highly processed and refined foods on the market today, many of them containing preservatives. They come in boxes, cans and packages. Some of the vital elements have been removed and in an effort to make up for this lack, man has added his own created vitamins and minerals. Our Creator's foods have been tampered with. Can man improve upon nature?

7. *Relaxation:* The secret of being able to relax at work or play is essential to both health and charm, and is an ability which is fairly easy to acquire. The mind controls the body and this control can cause either tension or relaxation. If you will merely *tell your body to relax* you will immediately feel a relief of tension. This same technique can be applied in getting to sleep when you are suffering tension.

8. *A healthy mental attitude:*

a. The effect of unwholesome attitudes: Worry, fear, anxiety, pessimism, hate, resentments, impatience, envy, anger or any other irritating mental images can have a detrimental effect upon the human body. Its destructive influence is carried by the nervous system to the entire body. I know of two men who died as a direct result of anger. Even after the temporary emotion has left—the physical damage may remain. A healthy mental attitude comes as a result of good character. If you suffer these unwholesome attitudes, it is a sign of a weakness in your character, and you need to develop your angelic side.

b. The effect of wholesome attitudes: Buoyant and kindly thoughts have exactly the opposite effect. Faith, optimism, love, kindness, cheerfulness, sympathy and enthusiasms all harmonize with body function, and tend to invigorate the system, and helps to produce genuine good health.

IF HEALTH IS BEYOND YOUR REACH

There are some who because of permanent damage cannot attain this ideal of abundant health. If, however, they maintain a healthy mental attitude, they may appear much more healthy than they actually are. Elizabeth Barrett Browning was an invalid, yet one of the truly charming women in history. Her husband, Robert Browning, adored her! Her physical weakness was not an added attraction but she had an abundance of other womanly qualities which overcame the physical lack. Radiant health is only one qualification of Angela Human. If you have a healthy mental attitude you may still be a fascinating woman.

CLEANLINESS AND GROOMING

Good health is not the only essential in attaining a fresh appearance. Cleanliness and grooming are also important. The teeth, the hair, the nails, the feet, and cleanliness of the entire body are vital contributions to the effect of freshness. It would seem inconsistent with our ideal of Angela Human to expect her to be anything less than immaculate and well groomed.

CLOTHES

A fresh appearance in clothing is especially attractive to men. Such things as fresh starched collars, flowers (real or artificial), clean shining ribbons, polished shoes and clean, well pressed clothes contribute to a fresh look. Certain materials and colors appear fresh, while others are drab. Clean stripes, polk-a-dots, ginghams, daisy designs and animated prints suggest freshness.

MAKEUP

Men are not opposed to artificial allurements if it makes the woman appear more alive and healthy. In fact, your attention to these details only indicates to him your efforts to please him. Eye make-up and lipstick especially help to make the face appear bright and fresh which is the reason they were created—to charm men.

CHAPTER XVIII

Childlikeness

EMOTIONS

> *Except ye become as a little child, ye shall not enter the Kingdom of Heaven.*

What is meant by the Biblical statement, "Except ye become as a little child"? Doesn't it imply that little children have qualities which are precious, which we would do well to copy?

Childlikeness is one of the most charming qualities in the entire philosophy of Fascinating Womanhood. There is no other quality which will do more to emphasize the human side of you. Therefore, it is extremely fascinating to men.

Childlikeness is an extreme girlishness. It is a quality of sauciness, spunk, innocence, trustfulness and tenderness all mixed into one. It is a changefulness of emotion, from joyfulness to innocent anger. It is the charming qualities of a little girl.

Vague hints are made of this adorable quality in our studies of Dora, Amelia and Deruchette. Dora was "captivating, girlish and bright-eyed." Amelia had the tender emotions of a little child, for her eyes would quickly fill with tears. Deruchette had a "childlike prattle" and "she who was one day to become a mother was for a long while a child." She had the giddiness, vivacity and teasing playfulness of a little girl.

There are four ways we need to become more childlike:
1. *In communicating our emotions to our husbands.*
2. *In asking for things.*
3. *In our manner.*
4. *In appearance.*

CHILDLIKENESS IN EMOTION

What are the emotions which we communicate to our husbands? They are anger, hurt, disappointment, sympathy, tenderness and joy. If you want to be fascinating and solve many of your daily marriage problems, you will learn this childlike art of communication.

Childlike Anger—Sauciness

"Her very frowns are fairer far
Than smiles of other maidens' are."

What is childlike anger? It is the charming and showy anger, spunk, or sauciness of a little girl.

There is no better school for learning childlike anger than watching the antics of little children, especially little girls who have been spoiled by too much loving. They are so trusting, so sincere, so innocent and yet so piquant and outspoken that they are often teased into anger. They are too innocent to feel hate, jealousy, resentment, and the uglier emotions. When such a child is teased she doesn't respond with some hideous sarcasm. Instead she stamps her foot and shakes her curls and pouts. She gets adorably angry at herself because her efforts to respond are impotent. Finally, she switches off and threatens never to speak to you again, then glances back at you over her shoulder to see if you thought she really meant it, only to stamp her foot in impatience when she sees that you are not the least bit fooled.

One feels an irresistible longing to pick up such a child and hug it. We would do anything rather than permit such an adorable little thing to suffer danger or want; to protect and care for such a delightfully human little creature would be nothing less than a delight.

This is much the same feeling that a woman inspires in a man when she is adorably angry. This extreme girlishness makes him feel in contrast, stronger, and so much more of a man. This is why women who are little spitfires, independent and saucy are often sought after by men. This anger, however, must be the sauciness of a child, and not the intractable stubbornness of a woman well able to "kill her own snakes."

Childlike anger will not annoy a man, but will rather amuse him, and will prevent the dead perfection of her angelic side from becoming cloysome.

Do not think, however, that we should cease trying to overcome anger. In the development of our Angelic side we must constantly strive to be forgiving, understanding, and long-suffering so that we can acquire a kindly feeling towards our husbands. But in the process of becoming Angels, we are still human beings—prone to anger. If our anger is kindled, it is there, and what are we to do about it?

Anger

Anger is a very real feeling. It is an inner turmoil which feels like steam gathering in a teapot. If intense, it can become sickening, frustrating and even painful. What do we do with this uncomfortable feeling within? There are five alternatives:

1. *Suppress it.* We can, of course, make the mistake of suppressing our anger. But suppressed emotions can be seriously damaging as we have learned in the chapter, "A Man's Pride." Those who do suppress emotions tend to acquire a self induced numbness which dulls the sting of pain. But in dulling the pain it also numbs our pleasurable sensations, like sunsets, laughter, and sexual feelings. We turn the fire off from under the teapot, but in doing so we cause it to become cold.

2. *Release it.* We can blow the lid off the teapot and release our anger by using cutting words, harsh expressions and displaying violent emotions. This only heaps fire on the flame and can contribute to turning our love to ashes. It is not our ideal of Fascinating Womanhood.

3. *Self control.* We can tighten the lid on the teapot, by counting to ten, and holding the emotions tightly within. But this only causes steam to build up pressure inside. You may be calm on the outside, but there will be an inner turmoil. Such a trapping of emotions will cause you to hold resentments towards your husband which may last for long periods of time.

4. *Talk things over.* We can turn the heat down a bit under the teapot and talk things over. But this is an invitation for a man to defend himself, and if he is more clever than we, as he usually is, he will succeed in putting the blame on us for everything. It often amounts to a quiet, civilized argument.

None of the above methods of expressing anger solve woman's frustrations without causing damage to the woman, to her husband or a marital stir. The only successful way to respond is with:

5. *Childlike anger, spunk or sauciness.* This method causes the teapot lid to gently bobble up and down on the teapot. This is the

only response that is charming, and the only one that will bring a man and woman closer together.

What causes a woman to become angry? It is usually her own husband, for he is often a thoughtless being. At times he mistreats her, is unfair, or criticizes her unduly. I have taught you that you must accept a man at face value, and learn to understand him. But will understanding alone relieve our feelings of anger and frustration? Must we endure such mistreatment without expression? No!

What a Man Wants

A man doesn't want a woman he can "walk on" or mistreat. He wants a woman with some self respect and spunk who has enough pride to defend herself. He would rather see the fire in her eyes than a resentful, sullen, frustrated or crushed look.

We learned in the chapter on character that self dignity is an Angelic quality. But sauciness is the human manner in which you attempt to preserve this self dignity. When you fail to respond to man's mistreatment you lack both the Angelic quality of self dignity and the human girlishness of self expression.

I knew a girl who lacked such self dignity. Her husband mistreated her constantly until she felt she was merely a doormat upon which he wiped his feet. I taught her the importance of this principle which she applied very well. Later, her husband thanked me for helping his wife. He told me that all during their marriage up until the time I had helped her she had been "just like a little puppy dog, ready to lick his hands."

How to Acquire Childlike Sauciness

1. *Pretense.* The key to childlike anger is this: *your anger, your sauciness, or spunk must be mostly pretense.* By pretense, I mean that your fiery display of emotions are mostly on the surface; they are shallow; you do not appear to be really angry; it is only a little act. And although there will be a showy display of emotions on the outside, there will be an inner calm, or a least a pretended calm. Try ham acting.

2. *Purity of character.* There must be no bitterness, resentment, sarcasm or hatred present. If you have these feelings you will have to work on your Angelic side until they disappear. You

cannot appear childlike as long as ugly emotions are present.
3. *Acquire a list of adjectives* which are fitting for the occasion of
sauciness. Dora, in the story of David Copperfield, had this
charm. She had a few pet words, such as "you cross old boy,"
or "you cruel fellow" or "you hard hearted old thing," which she
relied on. Be certain that the words you use are complimentary
to a man's masculinity. Some appropriate adjectives are brute,
tough, big, stubborn, determined, unmanageable, obstinate,
inflexible, unyielding, unruly, stiff-necked, indominatible, in-
vincible, hard, difficult, troublesome, irksome.
4. *Exaggerate.* you can exaggerate both his treatment of you
and your threats. For example, say "You are the most thoughtless man in town!" or "Well, so this is the way you treat your
poor little wife who works and slaves for you all day." Your
threats also should be exaggerated as are those of little children
who say, "I'll never speak to you again," or "I won't do anything
for you anymore," or "I'll tell my mother on you."

A good illustration of using both fitting adjectives and exaggerations is found in the following illustration from David
Copperfield:

DORA'S ANGER

David had criticized Dora because she didn't manage the
hired help well, and because of this one of them had stolen
Dora's gold watch and fallen into further difficulty. He put the
blame on Dora. The hired help was a young boy, a page, as he
was called.

"I began to be afraid," said David, "that the fault is not
entirely on one side, but that these people all turn out ill because
we don't turn out very well ourselves."

"Oh, what an accusation," exclaimed Dora, opening her
eyes wide, "*to say that you ever saw me take gold watches. Oh! Oh!*
you *cruel fellow*, to compare your *affectionate wife* to a transported
page! Why didn't you tell me your opinion of me before we
were married? Why didn't you say, *you hard hearted thing*, that
you were convinced that I was *worse than a transported page?* Oh,
what a dreadful opinion to have of me! Oh, my goodness!"

If you will notice, she does exaggerate and she has her pet
adjectives.

REWARDS

This charm of childlike anger will amuse a man and arouse in him a feeling of tenderness because of your extreme girlishness. It will not annoy him.

Another reward is one which comes to yourself. You will find that occasions which formerly stirred you to anger now only slightly provoke you. The steam no longer gathers in the teapot, for it knows it has a means of release. You will find, if you continue, that you will *cure the feeling of real anger.* You will then truly have to pretend to be angry, in order to defend yourself, respond to his mistreatment, and display the human side of you which fascinates.

WHEN YOU HAVE A RIGHT
TO BE ANGRY OR SAUCY

It is only when you, personally, have been mistreated that you are justified in responding, as in the following situations:

1. When treated unfairly
2. When ignored too far
3. When insulted too far
4. When criticized harshly and unjustly
5. When imposed on unduly
6. When neglected too far.

It is only when *you* have been mistreated *too far,* however, that you have a right to be saucy. We must develop our Angelic side so we do not become "touchy" and we must be willing to be forgiving and overlook trivial offenses.

WHEN YOU DO NOT HAVE
A RIGHT TO BE ANGRY

When a man has failed in any part of his role as man, you do not have a right to express disapproval. Anything in his department is his own affair and is his to neglect if he chooses. He is responsible for his own actions and has a conscience to guide him. You have no right to interfere unless his actions are an extremely unfair imposition on you—and that is rare! Any attempt to use childlike anger in man's department *will fail!*

Purpose of Sauciness

The only purpose of sauciness is:
1. To give vent to unpleasant emotions
2. To communicate your thoughts when
   you have been offended
3. To be fascinating.

You cannot use this as a means of reforming your husband, or even stopping his mistreatment of you. You must accept him at face value. It is only a means of preserving your human dignity, and it accomplishes it very well. You will no longer feel walked on when you respond in this manner.

If he continues to mistreat you, all you can do is to continue to be saucy. But it is most unlikely that he will. And if he does, examine it more closely and see if what appears to be his mistreatment is your own lack of understanding for his responsibilities he faces as the man of the family.

When you acquire sauciness you will find, strangely, that you will look forward to the times he offends you, so that you can practice this fascinating art. You will soon learn to feel as little girls do, with all outward signs of anger, but no inner turmoil. He may even tease you into anger because he enjoys watching you.

The Harm If You Do Not Respond

The woman who does not express her anger, but suffers it can become sullen and resentful. This is a very frustrating feeling to her husband, for he can sense that something is wrong. He may feel like a heel for having mistreated her, and therefore it is a very uncomfortable feeling. He dislikes her for having made him feel this way.

Cure for a Man's Temper

Some very fine men have violent tempers. But if you could understand what he suffers and why, you would be more sympathetic. He doesn't become angry with you without reason. You may have hurt his pride, or trampled on his freedom, or stolen from him his right to rule his own children. Whatever the reason, he is provoked at you and it is a very frustrating feeling.

His feelings, too, are like steam in the teapot. He also has several choices to make. He can suppress his turmoil or control it, but this approach makes him sick inside and causes him to feel resentful towards you. He may know also that if he is harsh with you, you will feel crushed, cut or frustrated. When he uses this approach it makes him feel like a heel, and he may dislike you for making him feel so.

What is he to do with his pent up emotions? Knowing there is no acceptable means of release causes them to gather like steam in the teapot and build up pressure. This is the very reason some men develop violent tempers. But if you respond to his temper with sauciness he will not be afraid to come to you as a means of release. This very thought—this assurance that his release of tension will not be offensive to either of you will usually cause his temper to disappear very quickly. Two women told me that when they became saucy their husband's tempers disappeared almost immediately. You should, therefore, compensate for his mistreatment of you by this charming response. You owe it to him as well as to yourself.

COMMUNICATION

There are some women who say that they cannot acquire this childlike expression. They have tried and have become "stage frightened." If you find that it is next to impossible, then it will be next best to "talk it over." But do find some way to rid yourself of unwholesome emotion. It is destructive to marriage. Continue to work to understand men, and especially the chapter on sympathetic understanding. Many times when women are offended or feel neglected, it is due to their inability to understand what a man must endure in his working world.

Whatever you do, find some acceptable means of communicating your offended feelings to him: there must always exist a kindly feeling in the ideal marriage.

THE WOMAN WHO BLOWS HER TOP

Often women who have explosive tempers acquire them by the same means I have just described men do. It is a frustration which comes as an inability to find an acceptable means of expression. When such a woman adopts sauciness, and learns to become charming in doing so, her frustrations will leave, as with the woman who has been suppressing them. However, if she still fails to control her long time habit, she must work to improve her angelic side.

Criticism, When Guilty

If a man is critical, and you are guilty, it is only right to admit it. Thank him for reminding you that you were in error. Man, as your ruler feels somewhat responsible to teach you. You are in a different position than he is when he receives criticism from you. If you take it well, it makes him feel kingly. But if the criticism is harsh or unfair, you need to protect your human dignity by defending yourself.

There is a quality of spirit which some women have which is charming. It is an invulnerability! These women have such respect for themselves generally, that criticism does not harm their feelings. For example:

I was in the company of a lady and her husband when he criticized her rather severely. He told her that she never cooked, sewed, or cleaned house and that he had to hire a housekeeper to do all of this for her. Then he told her that she never even taught the children anything. But she sat there all the while, laughing. She told him that he was entirely right, and very soon she would turn over a new leaf and improve.

Hurt Feelings

We have been talking about anger. But sometimes it is a crushing or cutting feeling of hurt she suffers. An insult may cut like a knife, and when it wields its blow, it is there. What can she do? She can, if she feels like it, respond with sauciness. But at times the cut is too deep for this method.

What does a little girl do when her feelings are hurt? If she is disappointed, sad, or hurt, she may only pout. Or the lips may quiver and a tear or two trickle down her cheek. Or she may have downcast eyes, rub her foot along the carpet, and mumble a few broken words. Or if there is an outburst of crying, it is rather exaggerated, with sobs and a heaving of the chest. This is amusing and charming and arouses our tenderness, and will do the same in man if done in the adult woman.

Childlike crying is charming, but the cry of a woman who is deeply and genuinely disturbed can be frustrating to a man. If such crying is full of emotion the man is often at his wits end to know how to comfort her. In his desperation he may even walk away and leave her. If, however, her crying is the innocent, showy, heaving and sobbing of a child, it arouses a feeling of tenderness in the man.

If the cry is one of emotional turmoil, it is due to a lack in the Angelic side and indicates a need for character development.

REWARDS

Rich rewards will come to you if you learn to release unhappy emotions through childlikeness. Giving vent to your feelings will make you a happier person. Remember that human dignity is a quality of character, and childlikeness is your means of expressing this spiritual quality. Therefore, it contributes to your inner happiness, or your serenity. And there will be an additional reward in the tenderness your husband will have for you. By expressing yourself, you have done him a great favor. You have relieved tension in him. Therefore, you have made him happier and he will feel tenderly towards you. The following experience was related by a friend, and will illustrate:

SAUCINESS

One evening, while visiting my sister, two of my friends dropped by to see me. It was very late. My husband had retired and when I could see that the conversation would be a long one, I excused myself to see if my husband objected to my staying up late.

When I walked into the bedroom he was irritated, and said, "Well, what's going on downstairs?" I felt his attitude to be very disagreeable, so I lifted my head high, straightened my shoulders, looked to the side and said, "Well, I came up here out of kind consideration to see if you would object to my staying up late. But since you are going to be so hard-hearted and disagreeable, I *will* go downstairs, and I won't come back until 2:00 a.m." Then I turned quickly and swished off, and just as I came to the door I glanced back over my shoulder and could see that he had raised up on his pillow, half smiling. Then I quickly turned my head back and went downstairs, and I did stay until 2:00 a.m.

When I returned to the bedroom I felt kindly towards my

husband, for I had vented my feelings and knew that they were well received. But if I had not I would have felt mistreated. The impressive part is that the following day we returned to our home and while he was driving the car, he held my hand all the way home for 250 miles, and was especially kindly and noticeably tender.

Many to whom I have taught this philosophy know the value of childlike expression. Not only is it a means to vent feelings, but it is amusing to men, and clears the air for love to grow. Little children thus express themselves. This is the reason they carry no grudges. The following experiences may prove helpful in learning the art of childlike communication.

1. The Harsh Critic

A young couple were invited out to dinner at the home of friends. Since he had to come directly from work, she went alone, and was there when he arrived. When he saw her he said, "Why didn't you fix your hair, it looks terrible." Then as she walked across the room he commented, "I thought you were going to adjust the waistline of your dress. I wish you would take better care of your appearance." The poor girl was terribly hurt. I know this man and can say that there is nothing wrong with him. He is just male.

What could she have done? It was difficult in the presence of friends, but she could have responded in one of the two following ways:

Sauciness: She could have opened her eyes wide, raised her chin, swished out of the room, slamming the door behind her, hoping that he would follow. *But, there must be no bitterness.* When alone she could have said, as she turned her back to him, "I don't feel like speaking to you."

Hurt: Or she could have appeared hurt, with downcast eyes, chin quivering and a tear or two, pulled out a handkerchief, dabbed her eyes a few times and left the room hoping that he would follow. When he tried to comfort her, she would first turn away, still dabbing her face.

2. The Unfair House Buyer

A couple planned to buy a house. The wife's only request was that it be on a quiet street and near school. But when the husband spotted the home of his dreams, it happened to be on a busy street and a good distance from school. The wife became so frustrated that she couldn't even express herself. The husband bought the house, and the wife suffered such trapped emotions that she almost had a nervous breakdown. I know this man and find him to be perfectly reasonable and sensible. But his wife did not know how to deal with him correctly.

What should she have said? She should have stamped her foot and said, "If you buy this house you will have to live in it alone!" Such a direct revelation of her feelings would have been a relief to him.

3. MUDDY SHOES

A wife scrubbed and waxed her kitchen floor, and when finished, her husband walked across it with muddy shoes. *What could she have said?* She could have developed the same kind of little voice a child has when its doll has been broken, and said, "Oh, dear, see what you've done, see what you've done!" Good acting counts!

4. THE PERFECTIONIST

Many men criticize their wive's housekeeping, meals and home management.

What can they do or say?

1. If guilty, it is best to admit it. You might say, "You are right, I deserve your disapproval. In fact, I was wondering how you could ever put up with it. But please be patient with me, and I will try to improve." This will make him feel sympathetic and patient. But do try to improve.

2. If you are not guilty, but are married to a perfectionist, or a man who lacks understanding, then say, "I work and slave all day, just to make you happy, but you are never pleased. Oh, dear, what will I do. You expect perfection!"

5. THE CAR KEYS

While preparing to leave home a woman accidentally locked her car keys inside. Her husband said, harshly, "Why do you always make such stupid mistakes!"

What could she have said?

1. She could tremble at his harshness, as Amelia did, for Thackeray states that she "trembles when anyone is harsh."

Cast your eyes down to the ground and let your lips quiver.
2. Or she could "stamp her foot and shake her curls" and say, "What an old scrooge! My, what a perfectionist you are to think that I should never make mistakes!"

6. Ignored

A woman began telling her husband something interesting, only to find him looking out of the window with indifference. *What should she do?* Stand directly in front of him and block his view. Do as little girls do, and pat his cheek, or pull his ears to get his attention. You might say, "Honey, you are not listening to me." Or sit on his lap.

7. Success Story—Harshness

While leaving a service station a woman ran her car into the cash register. The attendant was provoked, but her husband was even more irritated and harshly criticized her in the presence of the attendant.

What did she do? When they were alone together, she shook her hands, saying, "You make me so mad! You're supposed to take care of me and defend me, but you were against me! I hate you, I hate you! I'll never speak to you again!" Her husband was very amused and said, "I guess it was worth running into it, to see you act this way."

8. The Tease—Success Story

When entertaining friends, the man of the house brought out some old pictures of his wife to show the guests. She did not have a particular liking for the pictures, and resented his showing them. She tried to rescue them, but since he was bigger and stronger, she failed. Then he picked her up, carried her into the bedroom and locked her in. His purpose was to tease.

What did she do? She pounded on the door and made exaggerated threats. She threatened never to speak to him again, told him she wouldn't cook him any breakfast in the morning, and then said, "I'll tell your mother on you." "I'll go to town and spend all your money!" The husband, of course, was amused. The children of this family were standing nearby and were laughing to see their parents quarrel in this manner. They told many of their friends about the charming way that their parents quarrel.

Remember: The only purpose of childlike sauciness is:
1. To give vent to emotions
2. To be charming
3. To communicate your disturbed, unhappy thoughts.

You cannot use it as a means of reforming a man, or insisting upon proper treatment. If he continues to mistreat you, you need to work on the entire philosophy of Fascinating Womanhood.

You command proper respect and treatment through the power of fascinating womanhood.

CAUTION!

1. Your sauciness must be mostly pretense.
2. There must be an absence of hate, bitterness, and resentment.
3. Use exaggerations.
4. Use adjectives which are complimentary to his masculinity.

Be certain that your anger does not take the form of a woman wielding the rolling pin, instead of the innocence of a child.

SEVERE MISTREATMENT

The mistreatments which I have used in these illustrations are rather mild and are usually due to a man's thoughtlessness or impatience. There are far more serious ways that men sometimes mistreat women. Some men actually hit their wives. Some men neglect their wives, never take them any place, are very stingy with their money and refuse to give them normal liberties. Some men rule like tyrants, take their wives for granted, are demanding of the wives and some men are unfaithful.

When men's mistreatments are severe, childlike sauciness is not the answer. The entire philosophy of Fascinating Womanhood must be applied to melt what appears to be "a heart of stone."

Often men's ugly and cruel actions are the woman's fault and are due to her lack of sympathetic understanding, her failure to appreciate and admire him, her inability to accept him at face value, to place him No. 1, or other things. When woman tramples on her husband's rights or his spirit, she can bring his ugly side to the surface.

This entire chapter is devoted to the study of childlike emotions, and I have thus far explained how to communicate unhappy emotions, such as hurt or anger. But there are other emotions which we need display in a childlike manner.

TENDERNESS OF EMOTION

The emotions of tenderness and sympathy are especially noticeable in young girls. This emotion normally carries into the adult woman and becomes a feminine characteristic.

You will remember that Amelia's "eyes sparkled, except indeed when they filled with tears, and that was a great deal too often, for the silly thing would cry over a dead canary, or over a mouse that the cat had seized upon; or over the end of a novel, were it ever so stupid."

This tender emotion should never be suppressed in the adult woman, for it is charming to men. Have you ever felt almost to the point of tears during a movie, and then consciously tried to suppress the intense feeling because of embarrassment? Women tend to lose this charming quality because they try deliberately to suppress it.

CHANGEFULNESS OF EMOTIONS

I have seen little girls run into the house with tears streaming down their little faces, then at their mother's kiss or comforting reward, see them burst into a smile while the tears were not yet dry. They do not stay sad for long. They never hold grudges nor are they sullen for long.

If you will watch children, especially little girls, when they hear an exciting story, you will see just such a sudden change of emotion. Notice how absorbed they are in the details and even develop into quite a stage of excitement about what happens next. They may sympathize heartily with the characters involved, be horrified and delighted by turns, and act as though they can hardly wait to see if everything turns out alright. This same changefulness in woman is interesting to a man and keeps her from appearing monotonous.

CHILDLIKE JOY

Still another emotion which can be charming to men is that of childlike joy. It takes very little to make children happy, and when they are, they show it with pleasant outbursts. I have a little girl who jumps up and down and claps her hands at the slightest hint of a pleasant surprise.

And doesn't a man like the same response in his wife when he brings her a gift or tells her of some pleasant event to take place, or does something especially kind for her? Does he want her to respond in a passive manner, saying, "That is very kind of you, and I appreciate it very much?" No! He would much prefer that her eyes light up, her mouth open slightly and that she act delighted!

Years ago, I knew a woman whose husband left her for another woman. Many things came to light about his disapproval of her, one complaint being her inability to appreciate anything which he did for her. On one occasion he bought her a beautiful dining set which she accepted as though he owed it to her. When a personal friend asked her why she was not more appreciative, she said, "Well, isn't a man supposed to do these things for his wife?"

Woman's eager response is a man's only reward, and the women who know how to respond with delight usually have husbands who pamper and spoil them. They often do things for them and shower them with gifts for the sole purpose of seeing their delighted response, often buying them things which they don't even need. But doing things for a woman makes a man love her more.

How to Receive a Gift

Knowing how to receive a gift from a man is an essential art of femininity. Not knowing is unforgivable.

The correct way: The correct way to receive a gift is either with childlike exuberance or real deep appreciation, depending upon the circumstances. The quality of the gift itself is not important. It is only the act itself, or the thoughtfulness in giving that a woman needs to recognize and appreciate.

The unforgivable: A very real problem arises when a man gives a woman a gift she does not like. Because of this she may make the mistake of returning it, exchanging it, not using it, or even criticizing it. These actions are *unforgivable*.

This can be overcome by appreciation of the act of giving, rather than the material object. The gift is of no real importance. The man is! The object given will one day be dust, but your response will live on in his memory. Therefore, it is only his thoughtfulness that need be appreciated.

Whatever it is, keep it. If it is unflattering, wear it. If it is unfragrant perfume, wear it. If it is not useful, use it, and all the time remind yourself and him of how kind he was to give it to you. If it is too objectionable, he will complain and insist you stop wearing it. Then you can take it off. But as long as he likes it, wear it, or use it. Other people's opinions are not important.

What if he doesn't give you anything? Should you be hurt, and think that he doesn't love you? Examine the matter. He may not give you anything because sometime in the past you failed to receive a gift with appreciation. It may be your own fault.

Also, it is important to understand that it is a male characteristic to be negligent about gift giving. Some men don't have any idea of "what to buy." If you drop a hint, they are apt to forget. And they hope that somehow you will understand their problem and overlook it, and not interpret it as lack of love.

Also, men have a tendency to dislike the compulsion of gift giving which has been handed us by tradition, such as birthdays, Christmas and anniversaries. They would rather buy something when they feel like it, rather than when tradition dictates.

It is best to try to understand your own husband's attitude about gift buying, and if it is difficult for him, remember the fact and overlook it. Tell him that such formal gift giving is not important to you. He will probably be greatly relieved, and will be more apt to buy something for you impulsively.

We have come to the end of the section of childlikeness which has to do with "communicating your emotions to man." However, there are three other qualities of childlikeness which are important if we are to become Angela Human. These three will be discussed in the following chapter.

REWARDS

Although childlikeness may be difficult for some women to apply, it is one of the most important parts of all Fascinating Womanhood, for it helps us handle human frailties (our own and our husbands). Sometimes little irritations, which are really molehills, can grow to be mountains in size. Childlikeness will "chop the molehills down" and turn what could have been pain into pleasure, as in the following examples:

CHILDLIKENESS

"When I tried a saucy response to my husband's thoughtlessness, he said, 'That was so cute, let's do it again.'"

CHILDLIKENESS

"I had my doubts about applying childlikeness, for I didn't think I could do it. Then one time when I was offended, I just stuck out my lower lip (just slightly) and my husband said, 'You look so cute when you do that,' and we both forgot what we were upset about."

CHILDLIKENESS

"My husband came home about dinner time, and although I had a lovely dinner ready, I had purposely not made the gravy, for I wanted it to be hot. He said, thoughtlessly, 'You have been home all day. The least you could do is have dinner ready.' I was extremely aggravated, but withheld my feelings and said with sauciness, 'You big, mean brute! I'm never going to cook another dinner for you as long as you live.' Then he said, 'Well, I guess that's your privilege.' I gave him another saucy look over my shoulder and continued with the gravy, but before I was finished he came up behind me and hugged me.

"In times past I would have sulked and not said anything, and he would have left the house and stayed away the rest of the evening. My childlike response turned what could have been a miserable experience into a pleasant evening."

QUALITIES OF CHILDLIKENESS

1. Communicating emotions
2. Asking for things
3. Manner
4. Appearance.

CHAPTER XIX

Childlikeness—

How to Ask for Things—
Manner and Appearance

How to Ask for Things

Our ideal of Angela Human is dependent upon man and honors his right to rule her and his household. Therefore, it is important that she understand the proper way to ask for things. I do not refer to selfish whims, but to just desires which are in every woman's heart which are important to her and for which she is dependent upon man to obtain. I refer to *things she wants to have, to do, have done for her, or places she wants to go.*

The Self-Sacrificing Wife

During an emergency a man greatly appreciates his wife if she has the strength of character to put aside personal desires for a pressing or noble purpose. But when there is no urgent reason, a man doesn't want a self-sacrificing wife. She is his queen, and it is important that she treat herself as one. He does not want her to place her children and their comforts and whims ahead of hers, or even his own. But many women suppress their desires for years, thinking it is angelic of them to do so, and not realizing that they are robbing their husbands of experience which would make their love grow.

Don't we love those whom we serve? This is noticeable in all forms of life. If we neglect a pet we cease to love it. Women who neglect their children find love more difficult. With these facts in mind you can see that you owe it to him and to your marriage relationship to see that you obtain your just desires. But *you must ask.* A man is not a mind reader.

The Woman Who Asks but Is Refused

More serious is the woman who asks in an improper way and because of this her husband refuses her. Although her request was perfectly justified and unselfish, he would not grant it. Because of this she tends to hold resentments towards him.

MISTAKEN APPROACHES

1. *Hinting*: She may ask by gentle hinting or vague suggestions, thinking that by doing so her husband (who is supposed to adore and cherish her) will surely be anxious to please his wife and surprise her. If he overlooks it, as he often does, she interprets his indifference as lack of love. This causes her to feel neglected and resentful. She might say to herself, "If he really loves me, why isn't he aware of my heart-felt desires?"

2. *Convince*: Or she might, in advance of asking, think up all reasons why she is justified in her desire. After being thoroughly convinced herself that she is justified, she takes the matter to her husband and tries to convince him. Sometimes he does give in, but not often joyfully. It is with the attitude of being morally trapped with no other alternative. But often, instead of granting her request, he tends to think of all arguments against its justification. And if the woman becomes insistent, he pushes back with equal force.

3. *Demand*: Because of the failure of the two above approaches, some women become frustrated, overstep their bounds and demand their desires. This is not our ideal of Fascinating Womanhood, and the man in this case feels trampled on.

WHY THESE APPROACHES FAIL TO BE EFFECTIVE

1. *Demands*: This approach *usurps authority* and naturally is offensive to the man who is the rightful leader. He may give in time and again, but not with good feeling.

2. *Convincing*: This fails because you appear as an *equal partner*. This lack of respect for his authority places the man in the frame of mind to say "no" often *only to show his authority*. He may be actually in favor of granting your request, but says "no" automatically. He seldom realizes that the reason he took such a stand against it was to preserve his position as leader.

3. *Hinting*: This fails because men are too preoccupied with their own problems to even notice the meek requests of women who appear to be airing whims. He often, in fact, does not even remember such a hint from one day to the next.

THE RIGHT WAY TO ASK

We copy the correct way of asking from little children—it is so simple that you will find it difficult to believe. Little children just *ask for things.* They do not justify, or explain or argue a point, for they are too little and dependent. They merely ask for what. they want. It is that simple.

A little girl will go to her father trustfully, dependently, realizing that he has the power to say yes or no. The very question "May I, please?" or "Will you, please?" displays her dependent attitude and at the same time makes a man feel like the leader.

When this truly feminine approach is used it places a man in the proper position of authority and also makes him feel more masculine. When he realizes this respect and freedom as well as your helpless dependency upon him, he is psychologically in a position to do the utmost to fulfill your requests. In fact, he would probably feel like a "heel" to say no.

How Not to Ask

Try to avoid the expressions "Let's do this," or "I think it would be nice if we were to do this," or "Wouldn't it be nice if we could build a bookcase in this end of the living room?" or "Don't you think we should enlarge the patio?" If you are really seeking his opinion, this approach is the proper one. But if you are anxious to have your desire granted, it is a poor approach, for these attitudes cause you to appear in either an equal or a superior position and invite an opposing view.

If He Says No

If you use this feminine approach and the man says no, you can count on it that your request has been unfair or selfish. In this case you need work on the Angelic side and try to discover where you are at fault.

You may have failed to understand his duties as leader, or his driving desire for status. Or it might be that your request is beyond what he can financially afford. Often a woman's desire is in direct conflict with her husband's masculine responsibilities and he must say no to you as a matter of fairness to himself and his family.

Another time he is apt to say no is when you have not been doing your part as wife. If you are selfish, neglectful of your home and appearance, and will not fix your husband his meals on time and have failed to become fascinating, he will not be inclined to bend himself to fill your just desires.

You Do Not Have a Right to Ask for Things:

1. When it is a direct conflict with his role as leader
2. When he cannot afford it
3. When you have been a failure as a wife
4. When it is selfish.

When It Succeeds

If you are Angela Human he will surely grant your request if it is within the realm of possibility. A man will do anything for the woman who becomes this idealistic wife. This is the *power of Fascinating Womanhood.* Many men have almost "broken their necks" to cater to the whims of femininity and have loved their wives more because of it. You owe it to your husband to see that he gives you your just desires, for he will love you more if you do.

In addition, your husband will be charmed by your request. It makes him feel manly to be placed in the position of granting. Your girlishness will fascinate him and arouse tenderness. The following experience will illustrate:

Success Story

After having been taught this philosophy a woman had the following to tell:

"My husband has been the kind of man who has always said no to everything I have ever requested. I remembered an old promise which he had made to me voluntarily and which he had carelessly never kept. I had never felt right about it and it was something which I still wanted with almost a burning desire.

"I went to him trustfully and in a childlike manner. I reminded him of the old promise, but I assured him that I recognized his right to say yes or no. Then I said, 'All that I have in life I am completely dependent upon you for. And this desire I cannot have without your consent. Will you please consider granting it now?'

"He acquired a most pleasant look on his face, and laid his pen down, for he had been writing. He motioned for me to come over and sit on his knee. Then he affectionately kissed me and said, 'Do you know how you make me feel? I feel like I am a big judge and that you are some poor young thing who has come to plead her case.' Then he said fondly, 'Anything that you want in life you can have.' "

When a woman has such an effective method of obtaining her heart's desire as girlish femininity, she is rather foolish to use any other means.

STILL ANOTHER WAY TO ASK—EXPECTING THINGS

There is another method of asking for things, and although it is not childlike, it is very often clever and purposeful. It is an attitude of expecting, but it must be done in the right way. An illustration of this is of Abraham Lincoln's stepmother, Sarah.

Abraham Lincoln's real mother, Nancy Hanks, lived with her family for years in a little log cabin with a dirt floor. She was a meek little lady and her husband, Tom Lincoln, was negligent and lazy. He never got around to building a wooden floor for her.

After she died, Tom Lincoln married Sarah. She was a very fine person but very different from Nancy. When Tom brought her home to the log cabin, she brought with her several wagon loads of fine furniture and home furnishings. She took one look at the dirt floor and said, "Oh, my goodness, Tom, I couldn't think of bringing all of my nice things in here on this dirt floor. I will just leave them in the wagons and you can build me a wooden floor tomorrow." And Tom Lincoln did build her a wooden floor the very next day. It was disheartening to think that poor Nancy lived all those years on a dirt floor just because she did not know how to motivate a man to action.

Notice that Sarah was pleasant but definite and placed a time limit on the task. With the furniture sitting outside, there was emphasis to her request. She was entirely within her rights. But we don't always have the convenient situation to make such a request.

The childlike approach keeps the man in position of leader and authority. It also allows him the joy of giving, and therefore fits into our ideal of Fascinating Womanhood.

WHAT YOU CANNOT REQUEST

Our ideal of Fascinating Womanhood does not ask for love, affection, appreciation or to be showered with attention. These things must be given freely or they are of little value. The object is to arouse in him a desire so he will *offer* you these things, and the way to accomplish this is to become Angela Human.

CHILDLIKE MANNER

The childlike manner is the motions or actions of a woman which appear in her voice, facial expressions, or any other motions of the body.

Dora had a charming childlike manner. Her delightful little voice and her dear little ways were not only feminine, but childlike. At times she would shake her curls, and point her finger at her little dog as little girls do. Her attitude was childlike, her mannerisms were childlike, and her actions those of a little girl. David describes her childlike manner in his following observation: "By and by she made tea for us; which it was so pretty to see her do, as if she was busying herself with a set of doll's things, that I was not particular about the quality of the beverage."

This manner of childlikeness we copy, again, from studying little girls. If you will watch a child "play house," you will observe many things of real interest. She does not hurry through her chores "just to get them over with," as grown women do. She plays house for the sheer joy of it. She sweeps, cooks, or tends her baby because she wants to. You cannot copy a childlike manner if you do not enjoy thoroughly what you are doing.

Very often when a woman finishes a household task, or finally gets her meal on the table, she heaves a sigh of relief. This is just the opposite of the manner in which Dora served the tea, or the way a little girl delights in playing house.

The delight a woman displays when she hangs up some new curtains, or makes her child a new dress, or cooks a favorite recipe, or cleans out her cupboards, or even polishes her floors demonstrates the inborn domestic nature found in the tiny little girl, and so often sadly missing in the adult woman.

GIRLISH TRUST

Your respect for man as leader, your trust in his ability to take care of you, your general attitude and trustfulness towards him all demonstrate your childlike trust and dependency. This attitude you display in your manner, in the tone of your voice, and in the words which you speak to him. And it is this quality of childlikeness that makes him feel, in contrast bigger, more capable, and manlier.

DISPLAY OF EMOTIONS

Although we have already discussed emotions extensively, it is important to realize that it is through a childlike manner, voice, expressions, etc., that we display these childlike emotions.

TEASING PLAYFULNESS

In Victor Hugo's admiring description of Deruchette, he mentions that she had "the teasing playfulness of a child." Yet so often when we think of teasing, we are reminded of a trait which is rather obnoxious in children, for it can be an annoyance to adults. Yet the teasing playfulness in woman can be an amusing charm to her man.

Why do little children tease? They do it to drive away the seriousness from each other. Children at heart are playful. To them the whole world should be fun. They hate seriousness. Teasing, which may arouse the fury of adults, is better to them than the dead, droll seriousness of some occasions.

The motive behind a woman's teasing is very much the same. *A woman teases to drive away a man's seriousness.* When Dora sensed that David Copperfield was going to be serious with her, she put her little dog's nose up to his and said, "Boh!" to "drive away his seriousness."

In *The Little Minister*, the heroine, Babbie, knew the charming art of teasing men. The Little Minister was very serious at times, and since Babbie had a few little ways which provoked him, and which he thought needed improving, he would at times lecture to her in all seriousness. But she had a way of changing the subject, for in her playful manner she would "make him stand back to back with her, to see which of them was the taller." This so amused him that he was unable to proceed with his correction of her.

Teasing playfulness is a means of responding when a man is cross, critical or disagreeable. If it is severe, it may stir woman to anger, and she will have to express herself with childlike sauciness or spunk. But if it is rather mild criticism, or crossness, which often accompany a man's "hard day," it is easier to lighten his disagreeable attitude by teasing playfulness. Women should be like little children. We should not like or allow our life to become gloomy unnecessarily. Life should be lighthearted and playful, and it is up to woman to keep it so.

Notice that both Dora and Babbie teased by trying to change the subject. In this manner they drove away the man's seriousness or crossness. If a man has something important to say of a serious nature, it is best to let him proceed, but if you can detect an unnecessary serious attitude, you can break the spell of gloom by teasing playfulness.

Teasing playfulness in women, however, does not mean playing pranks. This trait is characteristic of little boys, not little girls. At times, it might be fitting for men, but it is never fitting for a woman and it is extremely unfeminine.

OUTSPOKEN-NESS

Perhaps one of the best methods of displaying a childlike manner is in being outspoken. This again we copy from little girls, and not from unrestrained adults. I do not wish to imply that we have "unbridled tongues" or to speak too frankly, with little concern for the feelings of others—a fault noticeable in some adults. The childlike manner I refer to is one of being direct in conversation, and not evasive, "beating around the bush," making excuses and failing to come to the point.

For example, if you ask a little girl if she would like to go with you to visit Mrs. Grumbly down the street, and the child does not really want to go, she will say, "I don't want to." She will not hunt for excuses, or ask to put it off until another time, etc. She is honest and direct. This is the response a man appreciates from his wife.

If your husband is shopping with you for new furniture and is suggesting that you buy something you completely dislike, it is not necessary to explain your objections. Be honest and outspoken and say, "Honey, I just don't think I want this one." This comment will not only relieve the situation, but will be appreciated and less likely to insult his tastes than would an elaboration of your ideas. Of course, it is important to please our husbands in home decor, but in doing so, it is not necessary to accept items which are a clash with our own tastes. Always his leadership should be respected, and if he is firm in his decisions, even about such things as furniture, it is best to go along with him. However, most men want to please their wives—want them to have things they like, and will appreciate outspoken expressions of your desires.

CHILDLIKE APPEARANCE

The fourth and last quality of childlikeness which I would like to teach you is that of appearance. I mean by this especially your clothes and to some extent your grooming.

You certainly need not have childlike appearance all of the time, but some of it adds a dash and variety to your appearance that is refreshing.

The opposite of childlike appearance is a matronly look. It is important to avoid this appearance at all times. What are matronly styles? Our customs have defined them and you can easily detect them if you will observe the clothes which older women tend to wear. Matronly styles are too long, often blousy through the bodice, button to the waist, medium length sleeves which usually have cuffs. Colors are drab and the designs are small and insignificant. Older women tend to wear shoes which lace and which have thick heels. This, however, is sometimes necessary, but even they could perhaps include some youthful styles when they are going to be sitting during the evening. Matronly hair styles are usually those which are "out of date with the current styles." Young girls always keep up with the hair styles of the present day. Older women tend to be old-fashioned about hairstyles and therefore appear to have lost their girlishness.

Whatever your age, don't lose your girlishness by appearing matronly in either dress or grooming. I know some women in their seventies who dress as youthful as women in their thirties and forties and achieve a charming appearance because of it. This youthful appearance also has a psychological effect on the woman in actually making her feel younger.

To achieve the most girlish appearance in dress, visit a shop for little girls and study their clothes. You will observe, for example, full skirts, or straight skirts with ruffles at the bottom. Or there will be jumpers, pleated skirts, and baby doll yokes and lots of petticoats and pantaloons. Dresses will be trimmed with ric-rac, daisies, buttons and bows, or long streamers hanging down the back. You will see white collars, black velvet ribbons, bright, vivid colors, and strong contrasts with an occasional suggestion of humor. You will see dashing checks, plaids and stripes, but you will also see dainty delicate fabrics trimmed in satin and lace. Hats will be either dainty with flowers and ribbons, or they will be sailors with ribbons hanging down the back. All of their clothes are pretty to see.

Another place to look for childlike clothes is in the children's section of the pattern books. Many of these styles are repeated in the women's sizes. You will not lack for ideas if you study what little children wear.

If you think it a bit ridiculous for grown women to wear these things, try them in your own home and let your husband be the judge. He might not like them to be worn in public, but he will love them at home and for informal occasions.

Although high-heeled shoes are feminine, they do not suggest childlikeness. Therefore, for variety, add some childlike shoes to your wardrobe, such as black flats which either look like ballet shoes, or have a strap across the instep, or any of the other styles which are designed from little girls' shoes. Typical is the flat baby doll shoe.

The most girlish hair styles, as I have mentioned are usually those which are most current. For around the home, you can adopt an extreme girlish hair style, if you look well in it—such as long flowing hair, pigtails, pony tails, short with bangs and face curls, etc. Ribbons and flowers add girlishness to hair styles, as do also barrettes and bands.

In leaving the charming quality of childlikeness, let me remind you that it wasn't long ago that you were a little girl and all of these things came naturally to you. You can recapture this manner, these emotions and this appearance and make them a part of you. It will not only be charming, but will be a means of communicating with man. Childlikeness will make a man feel bigger, manlier and more like the superior male. It is this feeling which makes the quality of childlikeness in woman so charming to men.

Remember, if you are to be loved and treated like a woman, you must make him feel like a man.

CHILDISHNESS

Childlikeness should not be confused with "childishness," which is a negative quality. To be childish is to display the *faults* of children, whereas childlikeness is to display their *virtues*.

A childish woman will appear immature and self-centered. She may blame others for her circumstances, may fret when she does not "get her way," and will expect unreasonable things from her associates.

When we were children we felt that our parents could accomplish anything, because they were our parents. To project this unrealistic thought into adult life, however, is to expect *too much* of our associates. It is not a childlike trust, but rather a childish expectation. Childishness is not attractive, and may even be offensive.

CHAPTER XX

Summary

You now have the completed picture of what a man finds ideal in woman. There may be other qualities which men find charming, but they are less important than the ones I have covered. These are the qualities which are essential in arousing his feeling of Celestial love towards you.

CHANGEFULNESS

You do not have to be all of these things at the same time. In fact, it is changefulness that is so charming in a woman. A man does not want a woman to be the same all the time, for by doing so she becomes monotonous. One time you should be bright and joyful, another time gentle and feminine, and still another time saucy. Sometimes you need to be serious, especially in your sympathetic understanding, but at other times have the giddiness, vivacity and teasing playfulness of a child, and occasionally an air of bewitching languor, or the kittenish or cooing quality which I described in Chapter XIV.

And if a man is harsh, try the patient feminine response I described in the tale, "The Tiger's Whisker." If he is cross because of a hard day, try teasing playfulness. But if he carries things too far and mistreats you and you have a feeling of being walked on or treated unfairly, then respond with childlike sauciness. Any one of these above approaches would be tiresome to a man if they were used consistently. He needs a change, and you become a more interesting, fascinating woman if you are changeful and unpredictable, as the author Charles Reade comments, "Girls like to be coy and tender, saucy and gentle, by turns."

In your efforts to be fascinating, do not neglect the Angelic side, which is just as essential in winning a man's complete love. Your admirable character, ability to be a Domestic Goddess, and your deep understanding of him and his problems balance the human side of you and make you ideal.

There is perhaps no other single quality as essential as "accepting a man at face value." Others you may neglect from time to time, and he may still love you tenderly, but if you do not accept him you will fail to be fascinating. You cannot turn aside from this essential ingredient to love. All else will fail without it.

What We Give Up

You should give up any effort to change a man and give him his freedom to be himself. You cannot reform a man. And if he mistreats you, you can only give vent to your feelings through sauciness. You cannot steal from man his right of leadership, or his right to rule his children. The ideal woman is one who honors her husband, even against her own feelings or desires. Even her dreams must be limited to coincide with his role of man.

It may seem that we do a lot of giving, and it does not always appear fair. But it is by such giving, honor and reverence to man, that woman gains a strange power over men. It is the power of Fascinating Womanhood. It is when you give up freedom that you gain it. It is by relinquishing what appears to be rights, that you obtain them.

The power of Fascinating Womanhood is a power so great that when you obtain it, you almost wonder if you can be trusted to handle it with care. But if you attempt to use it unfairly, or unrighteously, you will lose it.

So what do we give up? Nothing essential! And that which we give is richly compensated. When we cast our bread upon the waters it comes back buttered. We give up only disappointments, heartaches, hard work, frustrations and discouragements. And what do we gain? We gain Celestial love. We enjoy flowers instead of weeds.

When you apply this philosophy and become the kind of woman a man wants, you become a happy, well-adjusted person. And this is what nature intended you to be. This is your glory!

Point of View

Women can make or break a marriage. It isn't that we are so much at fault as it is that we have so much power to improve it. This may cause us to ponder over the thought, "It isn't so much whom you marry, as who you are." With all the stress on our "choosing the right mate," it is often overlooked how much we as women contribute to that proper mating and the successful marriage, and how many difficulties we can overcome if we know how.

Many women, unfortunately, do not know how to make a success of marriage and have a false idea that if they are honest, kind and good and are good housekeepers and mothers they will be good wives. This is not necessarily true as we can see. I know many women who meet these qualifications and they are poor wives. Their husbands do not love or appreciate them and as a result, these women are most unhappy.

There are, as I have pointed out, many girls who make the mistake of trying too hard to be good wives. They are too servile, too willing to please and their husbands do not appreciate their efforts. If they would think more of themselves and take on at least some human dignity, they would be better wives.

THE CENTRAL AIM

I have said that the cornerstone of woman's happiness in marriage is to be loved, and this love she can arouse by applying certain principles of truth.

The most basic principles which you must apply in winning a man's love is to make him feel like a man. You do this by admiring his manly qualities, by making him feel superior in his role as man, by filling your role as woman, as mother of his children and as homemaker, and by taking upon yourself certain qualities, such as femininity, dependency and child-likeness—qualities which make him feel manly in contrast.

This consciousness of his manhood is what arouses love in his heart towards you. You become to him the one woman in all the world—the most perfect, the most beautiful, the most ideal woman in existence, regardless of your age or essential beauty.

If you learn the art of making a man feel like a man, you will learn the art of Fascinating Womanhood and will earn his deepest love.

It is also important to remember man's most basic need in marriage—to be admired by his mate. If you, therefore, give him constantly the thing that means most to him—*admiration of his manly qualities, achievements and ideals*—he will be more apt to return such giving by bestowing love upon you.

HELPS IN APPLICATION

I have given you a woman's philosophy of life. It may seem like an avalanche coming down upon you. How can you absorb it all; how can you remember it all; how can you organize it and apply it in your own life?

An effective way is to make a chart similar to the one I have here included so that you can have a picture of what you ought to be in one glance. Keep it in a secret place. Then take one quality at a time, study it thoroughly and apply it for a week or so. During this time notice your husband's reaction to your efforts.

It will be interesting to notice how differently he reacts when you concentrate on a specific quality than he does when you apply another one. This is because you arouse in him a particular sentiment. Some things will amuse him, some will fascinate and others will arouse a feeling of deep appreciation and worship.

When you have covered the material, try to get a total picture of what you are trying to accomplish by referring to the chart occasionally. There are a few ideas which you may need to discuss with your husband, such as "his role, your supporting role, and family finances." It is better to keep the rest of this philosophy from your husband. It is far more convincing to you of its truthfulness—its power, if he knows nothing about it.

Rewards for your efforts you can expect immediately. They will probably appear unbelievable to you. But don't be discouraged if you "back slide" and continually make mistakes. It usually takes about a year to form habits which will be of lasting value. But once you have a glimpse into the heaven of Fascinating Womanhood you will never be content to enjoy weeds. You may stand astride for awhile between the two—unable to reach higher goals, but discontent with the unhappy days of the past. But eventually you will advance to the higher goals, never again to "eat the crumbs."

It is important that you also understand that once a man experiences you as a Fascinating Woman he will not be content for you to be your "old self" again. Once he has *tasted the sweet—he will not be content with the bitter.*" Although this may appear as a problem in your eyes, it is really an added incentive for your improvement and will help rather than hinder. But it will make you realize that once you start on the road to Fascinating Womanhood, *there is no turning back.*

Perhaps the greatest encouragement in living Fascinating Womanhood is in reviewing the successful experiences of other women. I have given many throughout the book and thousands more have been written and told. Here are a few more to remember:

SUCCESS STORY

"I had been on the front lines of the battlefield of marriage for twelve years. I had fought daily for what I wanted out of marriage and it had taken its toll. I had battle fatigue, shell shock, nervous tension and I was bitter and resentful, for no victory had been gained, not even a small one. I was constantly losing ground. I felt like I bore the total worry, cost, and all the responsibilities of this war and our children were the ones —innocent ones—who were suffering. After twelve years I felt I just couldn't continue this any longer and it was then that I was invited to attend a Fascinating Womanhood class.

"Now I am giving up my war for peace; the tension and weariness are over; I'm happy and secure. I can again meet my domestic responsibilities with joy in my heart because I have shed those that were not mine. Practicing Fascinating Womanhood has given me more victories in four months than I had ever seen in twelve years and I didn't fight for one of them. They were given to me without even asking. I feel loved and cherished, and it is beautiful. Even my appearance has changed; my face has a new light, my eye a new twinkle and real joy radiates from my inner being. Friends compliment me on how pretty I look.

"Before, he was making big plans for building on—not to our home but to the garage—a "bachelors" apartment where he could get away. Plans included a fireplace, sliding glass doors with a beautiful view; a Jacuzzi bath, pool table, bar, colored T.V., etc. After F.W., he is now drawing up plans to remodel our house instead—including a huge family room with a fireplace, a new bedroom for us (he has been sleeping on the couch for six years) and a service room for me with washer, dryer and a place to sew and iron."

SUCCESS STORY

"I am happy to say that Fascinating Womanhood is so successful for me that as a result of it and prayer, my husband was baptized into our church last week. I have seen my husband transformed from an agnostic enclosed in a hard shell to a warm, selfless Christian. Six months ago he was a calloused cynic. Through my self-righteous attitude I had driven him to hate the church. I now know how to look for the good in my husband and there is goodness there I had never envisioned. Now he kneels in prayer with me each night, my hands clasped in his. Is there anything closer to heaven than this? Our children are happy now and our home is a place of joy."

SUCCESS STORY

"I must tell you that my husband of five years—whom I love very much—and I were separated at the time I was introduced to Fascinating Womanhood. After reading and analyzing the situation, it took me exactly four months to win him back."

SUCCESS STORY

"I'm so happy! I've had Fascinating Womanhood almost a year now and I can hardly remember how miserable things were before. This past week my husband had the whole house carpeted and he saved up all the money and paid cash for it. I'm so proud of him because for years he just spent money as he wanted, mostly drinking, and well, I don't really know where it went, but now he's so interested in our home and improving things for me. Tonight he's sitting out with our dog who is due to become a mother any minute. I'm happy to see his love and concern for an animal. And it's so good to know where he is nights!"

SUCCESS STORY

"Since Fascinating Womanhood I have been singing around the house again. It has come back automatically. I guess it is contagious because my husband was attempting to sing along with the radio the other day and this I have never ever heard him do before. He can't even sing!"

SUCCESS STORY

"I had been married twelve mostly unhappy years. I had the

"strangest" husband in all of married land. He did the "awfulest" things and had the "weirdest" habits anybody ever heard of. Nobody knew how I put up with him and even his mother had suggested I leave him!

"Then one dark day when I felt like I just couldn't stand it any longer, my sister invited me to attend a Fascinating Womanhood class. Slowly I began to realize that his peculiar ways were really only his reaction to the horrible way I was treating him. I went home to him and told him I finally realized how wrong I'd been all these years. I told him how much I wanted to change and be a real wife to him. Well, from that day, when I started accepting him at face value and found something to admire in him he started becoming "human" again. My mother-in-law saw the change in him immediately. She was sure I'd used some kind of magic on him."

Angela Human
"The Ideal Woman"
From a Man's Point of View

ANGELIC QUALITIES

1. *Understands Men*
   a. Acceptance
   b. Admiration
   c. Sensitive pride
   d. Sympathetic understanding
   e. Desire for superiority in his role
   f. Make him No. 1
2. *Has Deep Inner Happiness*
   a. A result of character
   b. Result of domestic goodness
   c. Accept ourselves
   d. Ability to appreciate life
3. *Has a Lovely Character*
   a. Self mastery
   b. Unselfishness
   c. Benevolence
   d. Moral courage
   e. Patience
   f. Chastity
   g. honesty
   h. Humility
   i. Self dignity
   j. Gentle tender quality
4. *Is a Domestic Goddess*
   a. Good homemaker
   b. Good mother
   c. Happy in role

HUMAN QUALITIES

1. *Femininity*
   a. In appearance
   b. In manner
   c. Feminine dependency in actions and attitude towards men
2. *Radiates Happiness*
   a. Cheerful
   b. Sheds joy around
   c. Presence lights the home
3. *Fresh Appearance and Manner*
   a. Has good health
   b. Appears fresh in
      1. cleanliness
      2. grooming
      3. dress
4. *Childlikeness*
   a. Childlike emotions
      1. unhappy emotions
      2. tender emotions
      3. changeful emotions
      4. joy
   b. Asking for things
   c. Childlike manner
   d. Childlike dress

Together He Cherishes

BOTH ARE ESSENTIAL
TO HIS CELESTIAL LOVE

The Angelic arouses in man a feeling approaching worship. It brings him peace and happiness.

The Human fascinates, captivates, amuses, enchants and arouses a desire to protect and shelter.

Relationship Between the Angelic and Human

It is interesting to observe that the four qualities on the Angelic side of woman directly correspond with the four Human qualities. For example:

Angelic

1. Understanding men has to do with understanding masculinity.
2. Deep inner happiness is spiritual happiness.
3. Character is the health of the spirit.
4. Domestic Goddess is the role of the mature woman.

Human

1. Femininity corresponds with the study of masculinity.
2. Radiant happiness is an outward display of happiness.
3. Freshness comes as a result of the health of the body.
4. She balances her maturity by remaining somewhat of a child.

The Angelic qualities are spiritual and have to do with what a woman actually is. The Human are mortal and have to do with what a woman does. The Human relates to woman's appearance, manner and actions, and are influenced by her general attitude towards men and herself.

ANGELIC
DO'S and DON'T'S

Do's	*Don't's*
Accept him at face value.	Don't try to change him.
Admire the manly things about him.	Don't show indifference, contempt, or ridicule towards his masculine abilities, achievements or ideas.
Sympathize with him in his responsibilities and his driving desire for status.	Don't use other men as shining examples.
Sympathize with him when he is depressed or discouraged.	Don't try to solve his difficult problems, but give him the courage to do so himself.
Have a girlish trust in him.	Don't doubt his ability to take care of you.
Recognize his superior strength and ability.	Don't try to excel him in anything which requires masculine ability.
Be a Domestic Goddess.	Don't let the outside world crowd you for time to do your homemaking tasks well.
Make him comfortable.	Don't be a perfectionist in your homemaking.
Have character and purpose to your life—and show it.	Don't destroy your feminine charm by unwholesome thoughts, harshness, criticism, etc.
Earn a place on a pedestal by building a noble character.	Don't disappoint him and fall off your pedestal by lowering your standards.
Work for inner happiness and seek to understand its rules.	Don't have a lot of pre-conceived ideas of what you want out of life.
Revere your husband and honor his right to rule you and his children.	Don't stand in the way of his decisions, or his law.

HUMAN
DO'S and DON'T'S

Do's	*Don't's*
Wear soft feminine styles and materials which make you look gentle and tender.	Don't wear masculine looking styles and materials.
Develop a feminine manner by accentuating the differences between you and the men.	Don't act, look, or think like men.
Be feminine around everyone you meet until it becomes a habit.	Don't ruin the feminine effect by harshness, boldness, criticism, or anything which appears unfeminine.
Develop feminine dependency, and need his manly care, or at least appear to need it.	Don't be capable and appear to "kill your own snakes."
Be efficient in your own womanly role.	Don't be efficient in men's affairs, such as leadership, making major decisions, providing a living, etc.
Learn thrift and learn to reduce your wants if necessary.	Don't increase the family income by working.
Radiate happiness and shed joy around.	Don't destroy your feminine charm by a gloomy, too serious disposition.
Work for the refreshing glow of health.	Don't appear unhealthy by wearing drab clothes, neglecting grooming and cleanliness.
Learn to express yourself when your husband mistreats you by childlike sauciness.	Don't suppress your wounded feelings.
Learn to be angry at the right times and not at the the wrong.	Don't let him impose on you, treat you unfairly, ignore you or insult you too far without expressing yourself with the charm of childlike sauciness.
Be changeful in emotions.	Don't be unemotional.
Be exuberant in your joy when he does things for you.	Don't take things for granted and expect a lot without appreciation.
Do get the things you want out of life and let him spoil you, as long as it is not an imposition on him and others.	Don't suppress your desires unless they are selfish.
Acquire a childlike manner.	
Include some childlike clothes in your wardrobe.	Don't appear matronly or motherly towards your husband.
	Don't wear matronly styles.
Be changeful—unpredictable, and thereby make yourself an interesting woman.	Don't be the same all the time.
Reach out for the high level of married happiness by seeking to understand eternal laws upon which it is based.	Don't be content with anything mediocre in marriage.

There is in this world no function more important than that of being charming—to shed joy around—to cast light upon dark days. Is not this to render a service?
—Victor Hugo